Just As You Are: Buddhism for Foolish Beings

Just As You Are
Buddhism for Foolish Beings

Kaspalita Thompson & Satya Robyn

Woodsmoke Press

Malvern, UK
2015

Just As You Are: Buddhism for Foolish Beings
ISBN 978-0-9931317-1-4

Published by Woodsmoke Press 2015

Cover: Sanghamitra Adrian Thompson
Interior Design: Kaspalita Thompson

Woodsmoke Press
Amida Mandala
34 Worcester Road
Malvern
WR14 4AA

kaspa@woodsmokepress.com
www.woodsmokepress.com

For Dharmavidya
Transmitter of the precious Dharma

CONTENTS

Practice

Appendices

We're all fools, all the time. It's just we're a different kind each day. We think, I'm not a fool today. I've learned my lesson. I was a fool yesterday but not this morning. Then tomorrow we find out that, yes, we were a fool today too. I think the only way we can grow and get on in this world is to accept the fact we're not perfect and live accordingly.

Ray Bradbury

Love. Of all things least illusory.

Franz Wright

Foreword

The way is simple, only our hearts are over full and complicated. The Buddhas shine a great light and bathe us in love, only we are too preoccupied to notice. Yet, even though we wander about in self-imposed darkness, the love does not cease.

The beauty of Pureland Buddhism is that it points out this simple truth and invites us to rejoice in it. Rejoicing in it we find something of inestimable value to rely upon that we had not suspected or realised was there. We call this by the name Amida because it is beyond measurement. Somehow it is also personal, enfolding us in a great love.

Here we find a kind of generic religion. Though it comes from an age old tradition, here there is nothing exclusive. The light shines on all. Our very scriptures enjoin us to support all who have faith, whether of our form or not. Is this not how it should be? When all faiths practise love toward one another, shall not this world be a finer place? Surely this is obvious. Yet the simplest truths sometimes seem to be the hardest to realise.

There is no need for everybody to belong to the same group. Each faith community can make its own special contribution. Not all faiths are the same. If a faith brings love, wisdom, compassion and joy it is probably a good one. If it brings the contrary, leave it alone. However, we are all human with all the failings and vulnerabilities of our kind.

The path, therefore, should also bring deep reassurance and help.

Here two good people have written a lovely book about faith and practice. It explains their own journey and many aspects of Pureland. This is a wonderful contribution to the growth of Sangha community. It explains things in terms that many people will find easy to understand.

Buddhas come to a world and shed compassion wherever they go. When we are touched by it we are changed, uplifted and liberated. Something deep inside feels acknowledged and relaxes. Inner struggle abates, and ceases to drain our energy. We find faith, courage and vitality. Fears and worries drop away. Everybody has faith of some kind, but often it is scattered and invested in unworthy things. Taking refuge in Buddhas cuts through troubles. Peace within brings peace in our world.

To take refuge one does not need a clear concept. It is better to feel it than define it. Even if you call it by some other name, nothing is lost. We are talking about a deep intuition that is at the core of what it means to be human. To enter heaven one does not need to know its dimensions, to walk the spiritual path one does not need to know special techniques. If one knows such things, fine, but there is no need to impose too many criteria. A few words are enough.

A simple prayer expresses all truth. All prayers are encompassed in a single one. In our style, the simplest prayer is to call Buddha's name. One call is enough. A million callings are only one call many times. To enter this way does not take lifetimes of study. The light is available already. It is not far away.

For this reason our way is grounded in gratitude. We are not striving for perfection. Buddhism has many descriptions of life perfected and if, one fine day, one is granted such an apotheosis that will surely be a wonderful thing. In the meantime, Pureland offers this simple path for those who are immersed in ordinary life, yet who have at least the hint of an intuition of some radiance from beyond.

If you did not have such a hint you would not have read this far. I assume, therefore, that you, the reader of these words, are searching for something. You want to add substance to something that has brushed against your soul, be it ever so lightly. You sense there a promise. That promise suggests that there is something more to life, or something different from the materialist helter-skelter. It beckons with the possibility of a deeper truth, a greater harmony, a real chance of universal love.

Acknowledge that hint. It is a precious spark. Tend it. Revere it. Be grateful for it. It is what we call the Unimpeded Light. It is a salvation.

This book will not give you a do-it-by-numbers self-help, pull-yourself-up-by-your-own-effort ladder to climb. It will simply remind you of the love that is already there and the refuge that is already at hand. It will invite you to celebrate it and to do so in company with others similarly inspired. In doing so, it will welcome you home to a place of peace where all is completely assured. Namo Amida Bu.

Dharmavidya
17th October 2015

Acknowledgements

Kaspalita and Satyavani

We are most grateful to our teacher, Dharmavidya David Brazier. He has passed on wisdom, practical advice and an intimate familiarity with the Buddha's teachings, but most of all he's role-modelled the tender care he offers to all who come into his orbit. He loves us just as we are.

We are grateful to all teachers, both those named as such and also those people we've encountered that have taught us informally, often without knowing.

We are grateful to Sanghamitra Adrian Thompson for making the beautiful image for our cover, for designing the cover and also for his proofreading and comments on the text and design.

We are grateful to Wendy Hall for proofreading the book and for being our first and encouraging reader.

Kaspa is grateful to John Suler, who posted the Zen stories online that first led him to Buddhism.

We are also grateful to all the Sangha members who have supported us during the writing of this book – by doing the hoovering in the temple, by sharing their stories with us, by teaching us how to be better priests, and by reflecting the infinite light.

We are bombu beings: all mistakes that remain, both liturgical and otherwise, are ours and ours alone. Namo Amida Bu. Deep bow.

Introduction
Kaspalita and Satyavani

The idea for this book first arose when we were asked by a student to recommend a book to introduce our style of Pureland Buddhism, Amida-shu.

Our teacher David Brazier (his Buddhist name is Dharmavidya and that's how we'll refer to him in the text) has written many wonderful books which we urge people to read (we'd recommend you start with *The Feeling Buddha* or *Who Loves Dies Well*). We thought there might still be a place for an accessible introduction aimed at someone who attends one of our services for the first time, someone who wants to deepen their knowledge of Amida-shu faith and practice, or someone who is curious about why we have been inspired to dedicate our lives to being Buddhist priests in this beautiful temple in Malvern. With Dharmavidya's blessing we decided to write it. Neither this book nor these two priests would be here if it weren't for him.

This book isn't a comprehensive introduction to the many forms of Pureland Buddhism found in Japan and around the world. It isn't a scholarly tome – although we have both found that studying the sutras and drawing on the experiences of many spiritual teachers helps us on our own spiritual paths, we don't see it as essential. This book isn't an attempt to convert anyone to our particular form of Buddhism. Our aim instead is to support people on their own spiritual journeys, wherever that may lead them. Amida-shu Buddhism works for us but it won't work for everyone and, in our experience, it can be a bit of an acquired taste.

We are ordained Buddhist priests in what is known as Amida-shu or the Amida School of Buddhism. Amida-shu is a group of people who have committed themselves to this form of Pureland Buddhism. There are School members (people who have ordinary jobs and lives and see themselves as inspired by this form of Buddhism) and there are members of the Order of Amida Buddha, known as the Amida Order. Members of the Amida Order are those who, like us, feel inspired to take responsibility for holding the light of the Dharma in the world. We have both lay and ordained Order members. Ordained members are priests supported by the precepts they take at ordination. Lay Order members (also known as mitras) do not take precepts or act as priests but take some responsibility for the continuation of the Amida-shu.

The Order came into being in 1998 when three people took bodhisattva vows with Dharmavidya. Compared to most Buddhist schools we are still a young group. Initially these ordinations were carried out to allow the people taking vows to affirm and support their commitment to full time Buddhist training in a socially engaged context. As the years went on and more people became interested in joining this group and learning Pureland teachings, the Amida-shu evolved.

This book is written from our own personal experience of spirituality and of Pureland Buddhism. We don't expect that all Buddhists will agree with what we've written. We don't always agree with each other! We feel that each of us needs to develop our own relationship with spirituality, testing what we are told against our own experiences, and listening carefully to those who are ahead of us on the path.

We are wondering about you, reader. Maybe you already have a long history of practice as a Buddhist or in another tradition. Maybe you see yourself as a spiritual person or a seeker, or you might be a confirmed atheist. Maybe you want to find out more about Pureland Buddhism, or maybe you have a burning question which you'll be carrying through this book with you. Maybe you're seeking comfort; or maybe you simply want to read some stories about our lives here in the temple with our three cats and our vegetable patch. Whatever it is that brings you here – we're glad that you're here.

If through reading this book you are inspired by Amitabha Buddha, the Buddha that we have a special relationship with as Pureland Buddhists, you may want to do more exploration by following the pointers at the back of this book. Maybe you'll find one or two meditation practices that suit you and that you can incorporate into your current practice. Maybe you'll find a different perspective on a problem or existential dilemma.

Whoever you are and wherever you are, we hope that this book will support you on your spiritual path, whether you've been travelling it for many years, or if you're just considering a first step into the unknown. We have been graced with energy, courage, direction, joy and comfort from our travels with Amitabha Buddha. We hope you might find some gifts of your own here – whatever it is you most need.

There is a very deep love soaked into these words. It didn't come from us – we're just passing it on.

Kaspalita and Satyavani
Priests of the Amida Order

Satyavani

If you had told me a decade ago that at the age of forty I would be a Buddhist priest, running a temple and with a religious practice at the centre of my life, I would have laughed in disbelief. And yet, here I am. What happened?

There was no dramatic conversion. Instead I had a series of experiences that gradually turned me around and pointed me in an entirely different direction. I will speak about some of these experiences in this book. Some, like attending a twelve-step programme or falling in love with a Buddhist monk, were pretty powerful – but most of them were less dramatic, like reading a few key books and spending some time with a Buddhist nun who I thought was lovely.

I work as a psychotherapist. I have a decade and a half's experience of accompanying others as they venture into their inner worlds – often the most terrifying and intimate and joyful and surprising of terrains. I also write novels and bring my fictional characters to life, almost transcribing their stories as they flow through me. I am interested in bringing dark secrets out into the fresh air. I encourage myself and others to be honest about our fallible natures and like Augusten Burroughs I would characterise myself as '...made entirely of flaws, stitched together with good intentions.'[1] I love growing things, eating vegan cake, staring at the sky and bringing people together. I don't like spicy food, slugs or holidays. On good days I am cheerful, hard-working and curious. On bad days I am driven by fear and prone to trying to control others and the world. This is some of the prism that I look through when I see Buddhism and everything else – what you read here will be filtered through my personal history, however much I try to take a clear view.

I have ended up in exactly the place I want to be. I could hardly have dreamed of living in a place like this and doing the things I get to do every day. My life is infinitely richer and steadier. I hope that, through reading this book, you will get better at tuning in to the experiences that are turning you around and showing you something new. You may end up becoming a Quaker, or a White Witch, or just someone who sits and listens to the birds for ten minutes every day. I don't mind what, as long as it helps you to become a more loving person. Love is what it's all about.

When new people arrive on the doorstep of our temple, I particularly enjoy saying 'welcome' and inviting them to step into the shrine room for the first time. I've got the same feeling now. Welcome. Come inside!

---

[1] Burroughs, Augusten *Magical Thinking: True Stories* (2006) Atlantic Books

Kaspalita

Unlike Satya, a decade ago I knew that I wanted to be a Buddhist priest running my own temple.

At the end of the summer, exactly ten years ago, I was sitting on a bench on the promenade at Aberystwyth, looking out to the sun slowly dropping over the horizon and talking to a friend about the future. We had both just finished a Teaching English as a Foreign Language course which had brought us to that moment on the bench.

My friend was Japanese and I have some vague memory that she was already teaching English in Japan, but had come over to see how we did things, or to give us an idea of how they did things over there. She was looking forward to going home and teaching again. I was wondering what to do with the rest of my life.

In the twelve months before that conversation I had been diving more deeply into Buddhism. I was meditating regularly rather than sporadically, I was keeping a blog about my experience of practice and connecting with other western Buddhists, and I was studying books and talks by Dainin Katagiri and Shunryu Suzuki.

Despite all that, ordination still felt like a strange thing to aspire to. But of all the things I had done in my life so far, working in IT, studying Drama, and now teaching English, Buddhism was the thing that spoke to me the most and which seemed to offer me the greatest chance of happiness. The practices I'd been doing and the teachings I'd been digesting had given me a glimmer of light that I'd not seen before, or at least for a long time.

If most people had asked me what I wanted to do with my future I would have said that I didn't know, or talked about something in the theatre perhaps. But when my Japanese friend asked me I said that I wanted to practice and teach the Dharma.

'Why would anyone want to do that?' she said. What I didn't know at the time was that Buddhism in Japan has about as much relevance for young people as the Church of England does to most young people in the UK.

I pushed the idea to one side and went about trying to make an 'ordinary' life for myself. I kept practising Zen Buddhism, I worked in retail, I directed plays and sometimes I hung out at a Tibetan temple not far from my parents' house. They were the only real life Buddhists I could find at the time.

The strange iconography and the devotional aspects in the Tibetan centre put me off their practices at first, but over the course of a few months my home practice changed. I created a shrine in my bedroom and did my sitting practice looking at the Buddha rather than facing a blank wall, and at some point, without really thinking about it, my morning practice changed from a twenty minute meditation to doing three prostrations before the shrine. I told myself at the time that this was because three prostrations take less time than twenty minutes of zazen, and that I enjoyed having a lie-in, but looking back I'm sure there was something more at work. A devotional practice was sneaking up on me.

In 2006 I found myself on a psychotherapy course at the Buddhist House in Narborough (where I met Satya, when she came on the same course a few years later). Every morning there was a Pureland Buddhist service. I didn't know what was going on exactly, but there were bits I recognised from other places and the spirit of the practice felt good.

On the Monday evening of the course there was a sutra study group. Dharmavidya was giving a talk on the Lotus Sutra. His face was lit up as he was talking and he seemed to understand the deep meaning of the text. I had a moment of certainty. I knew that I wanted to be closer to this teacher, and in that moment I felt that *nirvana* (or the Pure Land) was close at hand.

That was the beginning of my journey in Amida Buddhism, which has led me to be here, running a temple on the Malvern Hills with my wife, and wondering how to transmit something of the spirit of our practice to you.

Take what you like and leave the rest
Satyavani

When my dad was a young man at college he shaved off the left half of his moustache one morning as a practical joke. Throughout the day, nobody mentioned it. When he pointed it out to people that evening they laughed in disbelief and wondered at how they hadn't noticed what had been staring them right in the face.

Our brains are wired to notice the things that make sense to us (or the things that prop up our identity) and ignore the things that don't. When people saw half a moustache it just didn't compute, and so their brains filled in the other half as a way of backing away from something that seemed unbelievable. We experience a kind of distress or pressure when we try to hold onto two pieces of information that seem to contradict each other. This is also known as cognitive dissonance, and it is particularly uncomfortable when we receive new information that contradicts what we think we know about ourselves. If we are praised for our creativity in the kitchen but have a fixed view of ourselves as 'not good at cooking' we might dismiss this new feedback by thinking that the person who's given it to us hasn't seen things correctly or is just trying to butter us up. It seems that we would prefer to think of ourselves in negative ways than to suddenly not know who we are any more.

What this means is that we go through life with massive blinkers on – blinkers of our own particular design which allow us to notice certain things ('he criticised what I said because I'm not very good at my job') and ignore the ones that don't fit with our view of ourselves or the world ('I can't take credit for making the room look nice because I'm just not a creative person'). You are wearing these blinkers right now as you read these words. You will already be filtering what I'm saying into 'fits with what I already know' and 'doesn't fit or threatens something I know'. This makes it hard for new information to get in. One useful rule of thumb is that whenever you feel defensive there is some new piece of information or a potential new way of looking at yourself that you're feeling the need to defend against. Try and get closer to this thought or feeling and you'll be on the way to finding out something new about yourself or about the world.

In a later chapter I will speak about my experiences in twelve-step programmes based on the guiding principles of Alcoholics Anonymous. One of the tools I've taken away from this programme is a list of simple slogans that help guide me. One of these is: 'take what you like and leave the rest'. This slogan gave me permission in my early contact with the twelve-step programme to use the new wisdom that I heard there without feeling like I had to agree with everything that everyone said. If I had a strong negative reaction to what someone was saying I'd just put it aside and maybe look at it again in a few months' time.

We can approach Pureland Buddhism or any new philosophy, body of knowledge or spiritual practice like this. When we first encounter it we can gradually become fond of the bits we do like (a particular line from the service book,

12

the tune of one of the chants, a story that we hear, the people we meet) whilst leaving other bits for another day.

I was given further permission to find my way gradually by a paragraph from one of our key texts, the *Summary of Faith and Practice* (see appendix D):

> The primary practice requires only one essential: realise that you are a totally foolish being who understands nothing, but who can with complete trust recite 'Namo Amida Bu'; know that this will generate rebirth in the Pure Land, without even knowing what rebirth in the Pure Land truly is.

Without even knowing what it is? This made it okay for me to not know, and even to feel sceptical about this particular area of the doctrine (which at the time I certainly was).

There are still a lot of things in the Pureland faith that I am undecided about. I don't know what will happen when I die. I don't know if there is such a thing as rebirth. I don't know where the Pureland is, or whether it really exists. I still don't even really know for sure if Amida Buddha is there, or if he's something I have created entirely from my imagination.

What I do know is that keeping an open mind about these questions and slowly leaning more and more on Amida (which I have a very real and tangible experience of) has definitely made me a less afraid person. Less afraid people are able to be more loving, and as I've said before, that's what it's all about.

What I'd like to encourage you to do is to read this book with the same spirit, taking what you like and leaving the rest. Know that leaving the parts you don't agree with doesn't mean you have to throw the baby out with the bathwater. Swish the new ideas around in your mouth and take some time to wonder about whether you enjoy the taste. Experiment. Disagree vehemently and see where the disagreement takes you. Every new experience and every book we read has the potential to wake up some new part of us. I wonder how different you might be by the final chapter?

A first taste of Pureland Buddhism

Satyavani

What is Pureland Buddhism? This is a bit like asking 'What is a garden?' or 'What does love feel like?' If you ask a hundred different Pureland Buddhists, you will get a hundred different answers. This is because they will tell you what Pureland Buddhism is to them – emphasising the bits they find valuable or meaningful, or the parts that have been drummed into them by their teacher, and skipping over the bits that don't resonate with them. They might describe it in liturgical, metaphysical, or historical terms, depending on the way they prefer to make sense of the world. Of course, we will both do the same – which is why we also wanted to include some stories from our Sangha members so you can hear a broader range of voices than just the two of us.

Here is my answer. Pureland Buddhism is a tradition of Buddhism formalised in twelfth century Japan, but with its roots going back to the time of Shakyamuni Buddha (who founded Buddhism) two and a half thousand years ago. It places an emphasis on the inescapably foolish nature of human beings, and on the salvific powers of Amida Buddha through a simple practice which connects us to this Buddha. In other words, Pureland Buddhism is honest about our limitations, and offers us a paradigm within which our foolishness can be transformed into grace. Pureland Buddhism gives us faith and helps us to love more fearlessly.

I didn't know any of this when I attended my first Pureland Buddhist service, whilst I was staying at The Buddhist House run by my Buddhist teacher Dharmavidya David Brazier and his then wife, Caroline Brazier. I was there to do a training in Buddhist psychotherapy (they are both psychotherapists). During our nine day residential course blocks we were told that we were welcome to join the resident community for their morning or evening Buddhist services.

I joined them a few times, not quite knowing why – maybe driven by curiosity, or a romantic notion about what it would be like to 'be a Buddhist'. I didn't know what to do, so I sat next to Hussam and Helen, who I'd just met on the therapy course, and copied them. We chanted strange chants in English and in foreign languages, walked slowly round and round the shrine room, sang odd hymns and did prostrations, bowing right down onto the floor. Once we did something called the 'thousand nembutsu' where everyone says 'Namo Amida Bu' at some speed over and over again. It transformed the shrine room into a space clotted with bees, and the buzzing of chanting surrounded me as I made a small self-conscious noise of my own. How did I feel about any of that? I didn't know.

What I did notice was a difference between the students who attended the services and the students who didn't. It was a quality I'd also picked up very strongly in Dharmavidya and Caroline – a very deep and quiet confidence. They seemed to know something or get something which I didn't get, and I wanted some of it.

I can remember chatting with Helen and Hussam after breakfast, and hearing them use the word *bombu*. When I asked them what it meant, their description appealed to me immediately: foolish beings of wayward passion – all of us. They laughed at their own foolishness as they talked and I felt a sense of relief. Was it really okay to be full of greed and passion, and acceptable just as I was? I had no sense at this point of what it was that accepted me, but I was happy to take it!

This, and a fragment from one of the pieces of text we recited (...Amida will receive you, and you may fear for nothing, since all is completely assured...) was enough to keep me going back. They were the little hooks that kept me engaged for long enough for some of my scepticism and lack of trust to be worn away.

We are all caught by these little hooks at various points in our lives. Sometimes the hooks are unhelpful – we stay in a relationship for too long because we get a very small taste of something we are starving for, despite being given plenty of evidence that we're not going to get any more. Sometimes the hooks start out as selfish (we might train in a new career because we want to earn more money) and end up being motivated by compassion (we enjoy helping people more than we realised we would). Are there any hooks holding you as you read this book? Elsewhere in your life?

As I write these words it is 7 a.m., and in an hour I will be putting on my robes and running our usual Friday morning service. Later we are hoping to create our first veggie patch in the temple garden, and tonight we have our weekly community meal. Tomorrow we're running a retreat day called 'Just As You Are'. I'm glad that my first little nibble of Pureland Buddhism was intriguing enough to encourage me back for more. I seem to have developed quite a taste for it.

Steve is a resident at the Amida Mandala temple and has been practicing Pureland Buddhism for several years. He is an aspirant.

I found Pureland Buddhism through a twelve-step fellowship. After struggling with addiction, Pureland Buddhism seemed to call to me.

Pureland Buddhism is the first form of Buddhism I encountered, yet after much research, is the only Buddhism that appeals to me.

The main thing I like about Pureland Buddhism is simply the most common phrase I've heard since joining, 'just as you are'. After leading a colourful life, the fact that I am accepted, warts and all, makes my practice and my faith much stronger. I have no need to change to be accepted. But by simply aiming towards following the precepts, I become a better person.

My daily practice consists of morning meditation, simply asking for guidance in doing what is right in helping others, followed by silent meditation. I say a regular nembutsu throughout the day, followed by Nei Quan in the evening. I also attend service every Wednesday and as much as I can on Fridays and Sundays.

Buddhist practice helps me to keep some calm in the storm. The tornado that life can be keeps going, but while I practice regularly and try to live the best I can, I get the peace of being in the eye.

Buddhism is a religion
Kaspalita

I want to say a little about one of the ways in which Buddhism came west, and a little about my own journey from being a sceptical, argumentative atheist to practicing in one of the most devotional schools of Buddhism. I hope this will shed some light on a sometimes hidden aspect of Buddhism, and invite you to think about your own relationship with religion.

As far as I can remember, the first encounter I had with Buddhism was one lazy afternoon at work around fifteen years ago. I was browsing the internet when I should have been working (sorry boss) and I found a website full of Zen stories. I didn't know it at the time, but this website was a collection of *koans*: recordings of dialogues between Chinese Buddhist Masters and their disciples, or between one master and another, that were thought to embody some aspect of Buddhist teaching.

> A Zen Master lived the simplest kind of life in a little hut at the foot of a mountain. One evening, while he was away, a thief sneaked into the hut only to find there was nothing in it to steal. The Zen Master returned and found him. 'You have come a long way to visit me,' he told the prowler, 'and you should not return empty handed. Please take my clothes as a

gift.' The thief was bewildered, but he took the clothes and ran away. The Master sat naked, watching the moon. 'Poor fellow,' he mused, 'I wish I could give him this beautiful moon.' [2]

I guess there must have been some seed sown before that in my early life, or a previous life, that led me to click on that link, or perhaps it was just pure serendipity. Either way it opened a door into a different world.

There was something about those stories that suggested there was more to life than I was usually aware of. They suggested it was possible to take things in one's stride and to have a sense of peace and spontaneity. The characters in them seemed alive in a way that I wasn't.

I was nineteen or twenty years old, wasting my days reading Wikipedia and other less interesting websites in between occasional bursts of work. I was an atheist and although I felt intellectually secure I was directionless and rarely happy. The only bright point was the community theatre I was involved in. Taking on the role of someone else allowed me to feel alive: to feel (or admit to feeling) a fuller range of emotions than I allowed in my everyday life. But that wasn't enough. Something about those Chinese Buddhist stories showed me the possibility of a different way of being in the world.

They were Zen stories, so I read a little bit more about Zen. It wasn't a religion, I read, it was compatible with the scientific ideals I held on to strongly at that time; you didn't

---

[2] *The Moon Cannot be Stolen,* accessed 1/11/15
http://truecenterpublishing.com/zenstory/moon.html

have to believe anything, just sit quietly for twenty minutes a day, watching your breath.

I liked the sound of that. In fact, if someone had put Dharmavidya's book *Buddhism is a Religion* into my hand at that time it's possible I wouldn't have carried on exploring this path at all. Anything religious seemed at odds with my scientific worldview and I could have easily missed out on something wonderful.

Or perhaps I would have just latched on to Zen, which was being advertised as non-religious, and may or may not have found my way to Pureland later on. We can never know of course, but I want to underline that this non-religious Buddhism allowed me to take the first steps on the path.

After meeting those old Chinese Zen Masters in those online stories, I began an on-off relationship with Buddhism. About a year later, I remember calling myself a Buddhist for the first time. I still didn't really know what that meant, but it had hooked me in.

In 2006, I found myself at the Buddhist House in Narborough, chanting the name of Amida Buddha. I felt at home there in a way I had not felt for a long time, if ever. Something of the same spirit of those Zen stories seemed to be embodied in the people in that community: there was lots of laughter, they seemed more at ease in the world than I was, and they were happy to have me around.

I'd been to other centres and communities by then, but none of them had seemed like a good fit. There was something at The Buddhist House that resonated in a way I'd not felt before. It wasn't their practice which spoke to me particularly, but a sense of being accepted just as I was, alongside that moment of clarity in the sutra study group, when I saw that Dharmavidya was glowing with the Dharma.

I also appreciated the aspect of psychological awareness in the community.

Two weeks later I moved in.

I handed in my notice at work, bought some red clothes, and became a Buddhist trainee on the road to ordination.

There was just one problem. I was about to walk through the door of one of the most devotional and religious schools of Buddhism in the UK and I still thought of myself as an atheist.

I needed to find a way to reconcile these two views so that I could feel settled in the community.

Pureland Buddhism centres on the relationship between the practitioner as foolish being and Amida Buddha, a perfectly enlightened being whose influence spreads throughout time and space without limit.

The central practice of Pureland Buddhism is nembutsu: an ordinary human being calling out the name of Amida Buddha.

I really liked the idea of a foolish practitioner. I had been exposed to lots of ideals in Buddhism, but not a single Buddhist or Buddhist teacher I met had embodied those ideals perfectly. My experience of Christianity as a child had also taught me to be wary of ideals.

It was a great relief to see the ordinary nature of human beings, including Buddhists, being talked about so openly. I was beginning to get a sense that meditation could be used for repression as much as for liberation, so I was pleased to see people being interested in their shadows.

However, I struggled to fit a 'being of limitless influence' into my scientific materialist worldview. I rejected Christianity years ago partly because of the problem I had with ideals being talked about but not met, and partly because the more I learnt about science, the less plausible it all seemed. Subscribing to a practice in which I was calling out to a cosmic Buddha almost seemed like a step backwards.

Looking back on it all now, I think that devotional Buddhism took hold in my heart early on, but my head couldn't make sense of it. Anything that didn't fit into my materialistic philosophy wasn't allowed, and yet I kept taking steps towards a devotional practice – from my time at the Tibetan centre, to my own practice changing from meditation to prostrations, to chanting Amida's name at The Buddhist House.

Amida is a Japanese word that comes from the Sanskrit *Amita*. Amita means measureless and is sometimes translated as infinite. Infinity was allowed in my scientific worldview. I had an awestruck sense of an infinite or near infinite universe.

That was my way into the practice. I equated Amida Buddha with the infinite universe and grounded my practice in that. When I was chanting the name of the Buddha, I was putting my small self into relationship with something much, much bigger and awe inspiring.

Buddhism is a religion. When the Buddha sat under the rose-apple tree as a child and fell into blissful meditation it was not something he contrived using a technique, but something that happened to him. In fact he was clear that happiness of this kind could not be contrived or worked out. In English we have a word for this: 'grace'.

Years later when the Buddha sat underneath the Bodhi tree on his night of enlightenment, celestial beings and gods appeared to witness the events. It was a god that convinced the Buddha to begin his ministry, rather than to simply enjoy the fruits of his spiritual experiences on his own.

Buddhism talks of many lives and the spaces between lives.

The first time I read one of the perfection of wisdom sutras I had to put the text down. It began with the Buddha casting a great light across the land and many different beings appearing and gathering around the Buddha and Avalokiteshvara. Gods and angels appeared with the Dragon King and his daughters and various other ancient Indian spirits, demons and goodness knows what else along with the usual monks, nuns and laypeople.

It was too much for my atheist mind to take. How could something of value be wrapped up in such obvious make believe?

You would think that, having just had three years studying drama, I would be used to important truths being contained within less believable stories. I suppose it was something about being asked to take on all this at face value that caused me problems. There wasn't anyone actually asking me to take these celestial events literally, but that was what I was used to in the Christianity of my childhood, and what I had rejected. 'If the value of the text is dependent on these miraculous events being true then I'm not interested,' I thought.

Buddhism doesn't put the same kind of pressure on us to believe these things as the pressure I felt to believe in the miracles in the Bible as a child – but it does suggest that there is more going on than a materialistic mind might imagine.

For about a year after I had moved into the Buddhist House as a trainee, I kept trying to squeeze Buddhism into my existing world view. Amida was the infinite universe and the teachings on rebirth were metaphors for psychological states. Everything that I didn't like or that challenged my worldview became a metaphor for something I could understand – either that or I wrote it off as apocryphal.

I suppose there was a kind of arrogance in thinking that I knew better than 2500 years of Buddhist teaching and commentary, and that the only way it could make sense was if it made sense on my terms.

The personal process I was going through parallels what happens when Buddhism moves into other cultures and is probably inevitable, both for us as individuals and for the new cultures Buddhism finds itself in.

As Buddhism moved from northern India into China, there was a 'matching of terms'. There weren't words in Chinese to express Buddhist concepts, so translators looked for words that were close enough. Or they made assumptions about what the text was trying to express, so they translated it with that understanding, bringing their own biases to the text. They used a lot of Daoist terms and that gave early Chinese Buddhism a particular slant. There was some idea that because Daoism expressed the truth to Chinese mystics these Indian mystical texts must be talking about the same thing, and some of the subtlety of the Buddhist texts was lost. It wasn't until a generation or so later that people began taking Buddhism on its own terms.

A similar process happened when Buddhism came from Asia to Europe and North America. At the end of the 1800s when Buddhism was coming west, a large swathe of Buddhism allied itself with Modernism and the burgeoning scientific movement rather than western religions.

At the 1893 World's Fair, Dharmapala, a British educated monk from Ceylon, gave a speech describing Buddhism as 'free from theology, priestcraft, rituals, ceremonies, dogmas, heavens, hells and other theological shibboleths.' David L. McMahan comments that 'even a cursory knowledge of Sinhalese Buddhism on the ground belies Dharmapala's characterization of Buddhism as free from ritual, priests, ceremonies, heavens and hells; yet this sentiment is often repeated by early apologists and its echo continues today.'[3]

Dharmapala felt that Buddhism in Celyon was under threat from Christian missionaries and deliberately chose to side with the scientific movement in the West, which was itself beginning to reject Christian ideas.

For Westerners, a spirituality or philosophy which offered liberation without the trappings of religion was very attractive – so much so that many ideas about what Buddhism is are still shaped by that early publicity.

The Buddhism that I first met used these irreligious claims to hook me in, and that suited me just fine. In fact without my own personal matching of terms I might not be here today.

I think this is a typical learning process. Whenever we meet something new we try and understand it on the basis of what we already think is right. As we get to know it more, we see that it makes a less ideal bed-fellow with our old ideas than we first thought, and if we stick with it, eventually we begin to take it on its own terms.

---

[3] McMahan, David L *Modernity and the Discourse of Scientific Buddhism*, Journal of the American Academy of Religion 72, no. 4 (2004): 897-933

A year after I moved into the Buddhist House I was due to ordain as a novice. Before the ceremony I had to go on a one hundred thousand nembutsu retreat. This was five days of continuous chanting in a retreat hut at the bottom of the garden. I repeatedly said 'Namo Amida Bu', from the moment I woke up to the moment I went to sleep. Each day Dharmavidya would visit to see how I was doing, and I would tell him how many nembutsu I had said. I think I got up to about one hundred and twenty thousand recitations in the five days. Of course, it wasn't the counting that was important, but the continual reminder of the Buddha's presence.

I went in thinking that nembutsu meant turning my mind to the infinitely vast universe and came out thinking something different. On the afternoon of the fourth day, when I was sitting cross legged in the retreat hut looking at a photograph of an Amida Buddha statue and chanting, I was struck by a new thought. What if there was more to the universe, in the universe, or beyond the universe, than I had been allowing? This was a crack in my intellectual armour, and it felt like something from the outside had caused that crack. It was like a hammer hitting a bell and suddenly I heard a clear note for the first time.

When I came out of that retreat, I felt like the sun was shining brightly. I don't know what the actual weather was doing, but I felt a deep sense of peace and experienced the whole world as being lit up. I was pleased to see everyone, even people I was usually less pleased to see.

The Larger Pureland Sutra talks about the light of Amida being without measure, and unimpeded. For a short while I saw that light shining brightly.

I could have tried to explain that feeling away. Perhaps it was just how it is to come back into the world after five days of isolation. Or perhaps there was a new lightness in me because of some of the psychological work and the letting go that had happened throughout those five days (I'll tell you about that some other time). Perhaps it was a placebo effect – I thought something should happen, and so something happened.

All those explanations feel like reductions of the actual experience, and whilst they might have satisfied my old materialistic worldview they would have diminished the meaning of the experience and made it less likely that I allowed it to change me.

The simplest way of describing what happened is to say that my ordinary mind and my ordinary way of being was interrupted by love.

This is what happened to the Buddha when he sat under the rose-apple tree as a child. It's what inspired him to go forth into the world, and it's what he passed to his disciples in various forms.

It wasn't ordinary human love which inspired the Buddha – he would have stayed with his wife and harem if it was that – but a sense of unconditional love. He recognised that there is a love which does not measure, or ask for anything in return. He recognised that each of us is already lovable, just as we are, and having had this love shone upon him he reflected as much of it as he could back into the world.

This is why Buddhism is mystical – because it asks us to place our trust in something that cannot be measured, and that does not measure us, and to be moved by it so that we can love as we are loved by the Buddhas.

It is a religion because the Buddha wanted this love to stay in the world, and so he created a community around it, with rituals and precepts and dogma.

My understanding of Buddhism, and of the meaning of my life, has shifted. We make beliefs from our experience – and our experience changes over time. It's also true that what we believe affects our experience of the world. I prefer the experience of the world I have to the one I used to have. I feel more at ease and more able to love, which suggests to me that my beliefs are moving in the right direction.

I wonder where you are in your relationship to Buddhism? Are you just meeting it? Perhaps making sense of it through what you already understand, or perhaps beginning to wonder what it means to take it on its own terms?

Getting from A to B (Atheist to Buddhist)

Satyavani

As a teenager and a young adult, I was a proud atheist. I enjoyed looking down on people who had religious beliefs of any kind. I thought that they were weak and deluded. If they had to rely on some 'God' telling them what they should and shouldn't do rather than deciding on moral codes for themselves, I judged them as immature and lacking an ability to think for themselves.

While I was growing up, I didn't have any positive role models of people who lived spiritual lives. I wasn't given any positive messages about religion. I enjoyed the sport of debates with my R.E. teacher, but some of her Christian beliefs seemed ridiculous to me. I thought that religion seemed to cause most of the wars in the world. I went to a private school and I remember how personally betrayed I felt when I saw my Chemistry teacher Mrs Rogers, who I really admired, going up to take communion. I'd thought she was independent, intelligent and cool. What was she doing? At University, a Christian boy told me that my elderly atheist grandmother would definitely go to hell.

I clung onto these experiences of religion and they propped up my cherished beliefs. We were better off on our own, without leaning on anything. There wasn't anything there to lean on anyway – anyone who thought so was clearly deluded. It took a crisis to challenge my anti-religious anti-spiritual stance.

Anyone who has been close to an addict (or close to anyone who is in deep denial about any aspect of their behaviour) will know that if you're not careful it can drive you completely crazy. I had been struggling for many years in a close relationship like this, and it was very slowly dawning on me that all my efforts to change the other person were completely failing. Things were falling apart. I was terrified that this person would die, or that I would kill myself in the process of 'saving' them. In desperation, I reached out and joined a twelve-step programme (a group based on the same principles as Alcoholics Anonymous) which promised help.

The 'hooks' that kept me in that group were similar to the hooks that attracted me to Pureland Buddhism. The people in that group had something that I wanted. They were a mixed bunch, as all groups are, but amongst them were several old-timers who seemed happy, grounded and switched on. I wasn't any of those things, and I thought that if I stuck around I might get some of what they had.

It's just as well that I didn't know anything about the philosophy of the group before I joined as I never would have walked through the door. All twelve-step programmes are based on the model and philosophy developed by Alcoholics Anonymous and describe themselves as 'spiritual programmes'. I found the first step painful but just about doable: 'We admitted we were powerless over alcohol [or whatever else it is we're addicted to, in my case trying to control another human being] — that our lives had become unmanageable.' In other words, 'I give up!' The second step, however, introduces us to what is known in the programme as a 'Higher Power': 'Came to believe that a Power greater than ourselves could restore us to sanity.'

What was this Power greater than myself? It sounded suspiciously like God. I did some reading and discovered that Alcoholics Anonymous was started by Christian people who found recovery only when they gave up trying to control their addiction and completely handed their lives over to God. This is in fact the third step: 'Made a decision to turn our will and our lives over to the care of God as we understood God'. This made absolutely no sense to me, but I was given permission by the group early on to 'take what I liked and leave the rest' and so I just put this bit to one side and continued to learn all kinds of others things by reading the group literature and listening to people in the group.

As time went on various people mentioned their 'Higher Powers' when they shared in the group, which I found very uncomfortable. However, I noticed that the people using the phrase the most were the people I most admired and most wanted to emulate. I found myself a sponsor (a bit like a mentor) who helped me to work through the steps, and she admitted that she'd also been allergic to the word God when she first joined the programme. Over time she'd developed a relationship with her own Higher Power, and as this had happened she became less defended when people used the word 'God' and started to find wisdom in books and in people that she'd overlooked.

I thought I might as well experiment with my own relationship with a Higher Power, regardless of whether there was such a thing or not. I called mine Bob. I started talking to him before I went to sleep, and asking him for help. It felt utterly ridiculous and even now I feel a bit vulnerable sharing this with you. Regardless – it worked. I started to feel less dependent in my relationship, less hopeless about the future, and less alone.

My relationship with a Higher Power didn't go much further at this point, but I can remember having the experience of beginning to trust something other than myself – maybe for the first time since childhood. I very slowly leant into the solidity of the programme (including my very cautious and sceptical relationship with a Higher Power) and I found myself held.

My time in a twelve-step programme ripened me to a point where I was ready to let new experience in. When I attended the Buddhist Psychotherapy training with Dharmavidya, my experience in the programme helped me to keep an open mind during the Buddhist services. It worked away at my defenses and, as I opened my heart, I learnt how to take refuge and receive the blessings of the Buddhas.

What gratitude I have now towards my 'qualifier', the person who gave me a reason to attend a twelve-step group. They showed me that I needed help, and gave me the nudge (or shove!) I needed. If it wasn't for them, I'm pretty sure I wouldn't be here now. What gratitude I feel towards the people in that first twelve-step group, and all the books I have read, and all the conversations I have had, and everything that has conspired to bring me to the place I am now. I am now a person who puts spiritual principles at the heart of everything I do. Thank God!

Why do you keep saying Namo Amida Bu?

Satyavani

When I first visited The Buddhist House where I did my psychotherapy training, the students who attended the Buddhist services kept saying a strange phrase: 'Namo Amida Bu'.

I heard it many times before I asked what it meant. People seemed to say it when they met each other and when they said goodbye. They said it when they meant, 'Well, what can we do about it – that's life eh?' and when they dropped a mug of tea on the carpet. They also chanted it during the service.

'Namo Amida Bu', also known as the nembutsu, is a way of connecting us to Amida Buddha, the Buddha of Infinite Light and Life. Whenever we say the nembutsu, we are bringing ourselves into relationship with this Buddha. If we say the name of our best friend we immediately conjure something of them – their kindness, their cheeky sense of humour, their calm presence. It is the same with saying the name of Amida Buddha. When we say it, we are bringing him or her to mind – a being with infinite patience, infinite wisdom and infinite compassion. When we say the name we are spending a little bit of time with this Buddha and allowing his good qualities to rub off on us. We are stepping into his 'field of merit' where we can feel safe and loved just as we are, which will help us to become more loving in turn.

I have heard many different translations of Namo Amida Bu since becoming a Pureland Buddhist:

> Total reliance upon the compassion of Amida Buddha
> I call out to Amida Buddha
> Homage to the Awakened One of Infinite Light
> I bring to mind Amida Buddha

Namo is namas (or namu) in Sanskrit and means 'adoration' or 'salutation'.

Nembutsu literally means that we keep the Buddha in mind – nem is from nien in Chinese (smriti in Sanskrit) which means 'to keep in memory' (butsu is Japanese for Buddha).

The translation I like best is something Dharmavidya said: "'Namo' is the little, vulnerable, conditioned self calling out. 'Amida Bu' is the Buddha on the Other Shore calling back.' You can read the piece this quote is taken from at the end of this chapter. I can identify with being the very small and vulnerable self calling out, and I like the idea of the nembutsu both being something we say and something we hear and receive from somewhere else – a call and response. In the act of saying the nembutsu our call is answered, whether we can always perceive it or not.

In Japan the nembutsu is usually written, 'Namo Amida Butsu'. In the Amida-shu school we have shortened 'Butsu' to 'Bu' as, in Japanese, the 'tsu' is a very short sound and doesn't quite stretch into another syllable as it does when we pronounce it in English. This means we can preserve the six-syllable form which fits into many of the chants that are used in Japan.

It don't want to get too hung up on translation. What I usually say to people when they come to one of our services for the first time is: 'Just copy everyone else, join in, and come back a few times before you make up your mind.' It isn't so much the form that starts to sink into you, but something of the spirit of Amida (with the flavour of our particular Amida-shu approach). When you taste something for the first time it's hard to know if you like it or not. Saying the nembutsu or connecting with Amida Buddha might work miracles on you, and it might not. Read on, notice any resistance or feelings of relief that come up as you go, and see if you can hear the Universe calling back....

> *Dharmavidya writes:* What is 'Namo Amida Bu'? Namo Amida Bu is the Buddha prayer or nembutsu. 'Namo' is the little, vulnerable, conditioned self calling out. 'Amida Bu' is the Buddha on the Other Shore calling back. Whenever we conceptualise anything, there is always an 'other shore', a beyond.
>
> The act of conceptualising is a mental grasping that encompasses something and thus puts a boundary upon it. Amida is the boundaryless. Beyond the born is the Unborn. Beyond the self is the Measureless. Beyond our frailty is Amida. We have been born – we are here – how can we make sense of it? Human beings seek to make meaning out of their existence. A great meaning cannot be accomplished within oneself, however, but only by going beyond oneself. The religions in the world offer ways to try to conceptualise this 'beyond-self' experience.

Buddhism does so in a way that does not load us with dogma, guilt, or an undue metaphysical burden. Some metaphysics are an unavoidable dimension of any kind of spiritual reflection, but we should know that metaphysics grows out of the experience of existence. I exist. I see that I am a small and vulnerable being in vital need of help of all kinds. I call out. Namo Amida Bu. I call out to the unknown that lies beyond myself. It is the power that forms and supports me. In order to be a self, one must alienate oneself from the rest of the universe. With Namo Amida Bu we call to our other half – though, of course, the 'halves' are disproportionate, since I am virtually nothing and it is everything. So by calling the nembutsu, I recognise my own self assertion: I recognise both the strength and the foolishness of my project to be somebody – and I celebrate the fact that the universe is always calling me back.[4]

---

[4] Brazier, David *What is Nembutsu* accessed 1/11/15 http://amidatrust.typepad.com/ eschatolog/2005/03/what_is_nembuts.html

Juline is a Sangha member from an area of the UK where there are no other Amida-shu Buddhists. She keeps in touch with other Sangha members by phone and email and by attending retreats. She is currently a Trustee for the Amida Trust.

How did I find Pureland Buddhism? I did not find it – it found me! As Rumi said: 'What you seek is seeking you'. Disillusioned by a reductionist, materialistic outlook I searched for a new way of seeing and being in the world and with my experience. A way of being that:

- accepts the realities of life – suffering & mortality
- encourages life to touch and move us
- promotes awareness of how we react to life
- helps us develop compassion and kindness for ourselves and others

In Pureland Buddhism I found all of these.

Buddhism appeals to scientific minds in the West as it can be intellectual, analytical and rational in approach but this is only one side of the coin. Buddhism is not only head, it has a heart. The Pureland school celebrates and studies the heart of the Buddha which is wise, emotional, creative and kind. Some styles of Buddhism run the risk of overemphasising the practice of meditation which can reinforce concepts of self-power and hierarchy.

I like that Pureland Buddhism does not discriminate. In the eyes of the Buddha we are all the same and accepted as we are. Pureland brings a strong sense of equality and an emphasis on making the Buddha's message available and accessible to everyone. It does not matter if you are educated or not, rich or poor, whether you think of yourself as good or bad or whether others do.

I do a morning practice of yoga, sitting meditation and reciting the nembutsu. Through Buddhist practice and Dharma I realised I can be critical and judgemental of myself and others which is not helpful. With acceptance something has softened in me. My practice grounds me, calms me, keeps me balanced and steady – physically and mentally. Recently I feel a deep sense of gratitude for all I have received. I feel at home in Pureland Buddhism.

Bombu nature
Kaspalita

One of the distinctive features of Pureland Buddhism is that it begins by recognising that we are all foolish beings of wayward passion, or bombu in Japanese.

When I first heard the term and what it meant I was reassured. I had been worried that something was missing from Buddhist practice. Much of the Buddhism I had encountered as a beginner only talked about the ideals of practice, and bombu seemed to fill the gap.

One of my first ever Buddhist retreats was with the Network of Engaged Buddhists. The retreat was led by Zen teacher Ken Jones, and while I remember the whole retreat warmly, one exercise stands out.

We were asked to meditate in pairs. For the first half of the meditation one of us would sit in a meditation posture, whilst the other would repeatedly ask the first 'Who are you?' For the second half we would swap roles.

When I was on the receiving end of this question I had a deep sense of looking down into a dark hole, like an endless well. I remember feeling like I could go to the edge of that hole and look down but not enter the darkness.

I was looking into my own shadow. This is what Robert Bly calls 'the long bag we drag behind us'[5]. He suggests that as infants we are radiating energy from all parts of our body and our mind, and over time we learn that certain parts of our being are not acceptable to society, or in our family, so we stuff them into the long dark bag. Anger, for example, is something that many people stuff into their bags.

I didn't know what was in that dark well I was looking into, and I didn't want to know. Goodness knows what I might find down there, I thought.

Stuffing things into our long bags not only cuts off those parts of ourselves, stifling creativity and our ability to love and engage with the world wholeheartedly, but can lead to other problems.

The bag is not a perfect container – it is speckled with small holes and tears, and the more you push in the more stuff leaks out the other end. When we push anger down it squeezes through the holes and comes out as resentment or passive aggressiveness.

There was certainly anger in my bag, and sometimes it did leak out as passive aggressive behaviour.

As my meditation practice developed, I began to worry that I could use the practice to keep things in the well or the long bag. Every time I caught a glimpse of something about myself that I didn't like, I could just focus on my breath again, and forget about it.

There were lots of ideals talked about in the Buddhist books that I was reading at the time, like keeping the

---

[5] Bly, Robert *A Little Book on The Human Shadow* (1988) Harper Collins

precepts, always being mindful, and loving each other. These are all good things to do, but that's when I started to get the sense that something was missing, something about human nature.

I had seen people take vows before in the Christian church I was part of as a child. Some of these people didn't take their vows seriously, and didn't worry about breaking them. Some of these people did take them seriously but wouldn't have been able to tell you about all the subtle ways in which they were breaking them.

There is a danger in many forms of religion and spirituality that we become nice, or pretend to be nice, because we are afraid of looking in the long dark bag.

This worried me so much that I was starting to have misgivings about Buddhist practice. Then I read Jack Kornfield's book *After the Ecstasy the Laundry*[6], which spoke about human nature and how great spiritual insight didn't necessarily lead to perfect behaviour or a life without stress. The book, which I still recommend, is essentially a collection of interviews with senior practitioners and teachers in which they bare their hearts and talk about the difficulties in their lives and practices, difficulties which continued even after their enlightenment experiences.

You might think that reading about all their troubles would undermine my faith in the Buddhist tradition, but actually it was a great relief to meet this more honest, human side of Buddhism and my faith grew.

Not long after reading that book I made my first visit to The Buddhist House, and heard the term bombu. Some people take the idea of being a foolish being glibly, or worry

---

[6] Kornfield, Jack *After the Ecstasy, the Laundry* (2000) Rider

that it can become an excuse not to take responsibility for one's actions, but I understood it was an important feature of Pureland Buddhism, and without knowing anything else about Pureland, it gave me some hope that I might find a fit between myself and the tradition.

We can use the idea of bombu nature to excuse ourselves when we cause harm, saying 'Oh silly me, just my bombu nature again.' Sometimes, when we are just noticing that we are about to engage in one or another compulsive activity this light gentle noticing can be just the right approach. But if we use it to hide from the consequences of our actions when we have been unskillful or caused harm we are missing the point.

Recognising our bombu nature is a hard thing to do – it means really looking at what motivates our actions, and how we are compelled by greed, and hate and delusion. It means noticing when all the stuff we have pushed into our long bag starts to leak out and taking responsibility for that, and it sometimes means looking into the long bag itself and seeing what is there, in the darkest places in our psyches.

Since that retreat with Ken Jones I have looked into the dark well that I saw in that meditation many times. There is still plenty of stuff hiding at the bottom (there will always be something down there) but I have been able to bring a great deal into the light, to recognise when I have acted from spite or meanness or from wanting to push people away, and to see the results of those actions – usually unhappiness for others, and for myself too.

In my own case I spent many years pushing my selfish impulses into the long bag. Other people may act on these impulses more directly – instead of my passive aggressiveness their anger might erupt as soon as it arises, and so on. Those people might look more chaotic in the world compared to me, but we are all being selfish, just with different styles. We all have different ways of denying our nature too; some of us simply stuff the selfish feelings away, some of us might act on them immediately but then blame others or the world for the consequences.

Whilst I'm talking about the long bag, it's worth mentioning that what some people stuff down there might be their creativity, or compassion. It isn't necessarily selfish thoughts we repress, but whatever we have learnt isn't allowed. I'd encourage you to be curious about what might be hiding in your own shadow.

Whatever your own style of dealing with greed, hate and delusion, whether it is close to the surface or buried away somewhere and leaking out in subtle ways, it will be creating suffering in the world and for you.

The greatest sense of peace and equanimity comes when we are able to bring our whole selves, including our selfish impulses and actions, into the light.

This is why we put ourselves in relationship to Amida Buddha. He can accept and love the parts of ourselves that we cannot, including the most selfish parts of our bombu nature.

This process of bringing ourselves into the light also seems to take the power away from those selfish feelings. In my own experience, stuffing selfishness into my long bag ironically gave those thoughts and feelings a strong influence on my life. Now I am in relationship to Amida, I am able to practice emptying the bag. I will never empty it completely, or stop selfish impulses from appearing in the first place, but I know I am lovable, by the Buddha, just as I am.

The F-word – faith

Satyavani

Whether we see ourselves as spiritual beings or not, we all have faith in something. Right now I have faith that the keys I press on the keyboard will translate into words on the screen. I have faith that the floor will hold me up, and that the sun will continue to rise through the morning mist.

We take comfort from the things that we have faith in, or, to put it another way, the things that we take refuge in. Most of us in the modern world take refuge in material goods to some extent: money, possessions and the accompanying status. We have faith that if we do what society expects us to do – get married, have children, buy a nice house – that we'll live happily ever after. We think that if we successfully seek and receive praise and fame then we'll feel better about ourselves. We take refuge as a way of avoiding the feelings we don't like and clinging onto the feelings we do like, and we take refuge as an antidote to existential and other forms of fear.

We are especially fond of taking refuge in behaviours that become ever-so slightly (or ragingly) compulsive. We love the reliable feeling of relaxation when we drink our first glass of wine of the evening, or when we turn on the television. My own favourite compulsions are sweet foods, overwork, and social media addiction. When I feel sad or bad

I reach for sugar, regardless of how effectively it staves off the emotion. Sugar has been faithful to me in the past, and now I am faithful to it – expecting relief even when it often leaves me feeling dissatisfied and slightly sick. What are your favourite compulsions?

All of these places where we habitually take refuge (especially the ones with a more compulsive quality) are flawed. As most of us know intellectually, money or possessions can't make us happy. Research tends to suggest that after our basic needs are met, increases in salary no longer lead to increases in happiness.

One of the things that we are encouraged to do in Buddhism is to begin to take refuge in healthier worldly pursuits. We might swap chocolate for yoga or walking in the hills, and alcohol for an addiction to running. This is a good thing to do. Ultimately though, none of these places of worldly refuge are reliable. They keep shifting about. Our favourite yoga teacher moves away or we injure our knee and we can't run any more. Relationships change, possessions come and go, and people die. And so, more importantly, Buddhism suggests that we place our faith in something that transcends the material world entirely – something that transcends impermanence.

In the Amida-shu we take refuge in what are known as the five jewels – Amida Buddha, the Buddha of Infinite Light; Shakyamuni Buddha, the founder of Buddhism; the Dharma, the Buddha's teachings; the Sangha, the community of Buddhists and the Pure Land, the field of merit surrounding Amida Buddha. These places of refuge, especially Amida Buddha, are not impermanent.

How does this 'taking refuge' work in practice? Different people will find their way to refuge in different ways. To start with we might choose to take refuge in the Sangha, and to trust that as a group they will hold us in a way that would be impossible for any individual to do. We might trust that the wisdom we need will come from the Sangha, sometimes from the person we least expect. We might experiment with sharing more honestly with the Sangha – taking it slowly – and see how we are received.

We might take refuge in the Dharma by listening to Buddhist teachings and reading Buddhist books. Since Shakyamuni Buddha started teaching 2500 years ago, a great body of wisdom has accumulated from lots of different teachers in lots of different traditions. We might also try to follow the precepts, which offer us guidance on how to live a good life.

For me, the most powerful way of countering fear is to take refuge in the Buddha. To begin with I did this by copying what others did, especially my teacher. I wanted to be more like him, and so I did what he did – clipping the lavender like he clipped it, placing my service book on the floor carefully as he did. This is how we learn as children and it is a very powerful way to learn. We copy the people we want to emulate unconsciously and as we perform the same actions as them or say the same things they do, we learn new ways of being. If we are feeling depressed and purposefully move our bodies into a more upright, open position, more positive feelings usually follow. In a similar way, as I attended Buddhist services and moved my body into various positions – sitting upright, bowing – I began to feel some of the same faith in the Buddha that my teacher feels. When I look at the Buddha now, I know that I see something of what he sees.

At the beginning of our practice, most of us enter into a true experience of taking refuge through first trusting in those who have come before us – those experienced practitioners who have learnt how to take refuge through someone who came before them. This person-to-person transmission of the Dharma is a very important part of Buddhism. Deep spiritual experience passes like a benevolent virus from teacher to student, teacher to student, and if we are lucky we come into contact with enough 'infected' people to be blessed with the virus ourselves. Another word for this virus is faith.

What are the benefits of taking refuge in the five jewels? Since becoming a Buddhist and finding faith my life does look a bit different from the outside as I now run a Buddhist temple, but I still work as a psychotherapist and write as I did before, I still enjoy gardening, and I still struggle with my favourite compulsions. What has changed is that I am driven by a different engine. My faith lies underneath everything I do – inspiring me to connect with the Buddha and to become a more loving person, despite my fallibility. As promised in the *Summary of Faith of Practice* I do feel a 'settled faith', which makes it easier to meet life's many challenges head on and to find comfort when I feel overwhelmed. I think I take more risks now – I am more likely to speak my truth, regardless of how I guess other people will react, and I am more able to stand up for what I believe in.

I hesitate to make these claims about myself as I don't want to give the impression that having faith has 'fixed me' in any way. I am still a foolish being of wayward passions. I still make many mistakes, act from fear, am still selfish, jealous and greedy. If anything, since becoming a Buddhist I have felt safe enough to gain an ever-deeper realisation of how full-of-self I am – with the weight of our karma, how do any of us manage to do any good at all?

But through the grace of Amida, I do feel that many good things have happened as a direct result of me taking refuge. If not, what would be the point? If Buddhism didn't help people to become more compassionate and loving, why would I want to spread the Dharma? After becoming enlightened the Buddha did need a little persuasion to teach others (he was convinced that nobody would understand the Dharma), but he then went on to give a multitude of teachings to many different people over the next thirty five years. He made his best attempt at saving all sentient beings.

If you like the sound of faith, how might you get more of it? It helps when you try to get 'out of the way' – become aware of the defenses you might have built up over time, and see what happens when you relax them just a little. Find people who seem full of faith and spend as much time with them as you can. Fake it to make it. Find a spiritual practice that suits you, and a Sangha where you feel at home. Spend time on your relationship with the Buddha or a Higher Power, even if you don't know if you believe in it or not; ask for help; hand things over when they become unmanageable and say thank you. If you don't know what to say thank you for, look harder – and make saying thank you a core part of your practice. Having said all this, grace often visits us when we least expect it – we're not in control of it, that's the point! It is beyond us. We say Namo Amida Bu and we trust that '...all is completely assured.'

My faith comes and goes, as it does for most people. On some days I wonder what on earth I am doing, or I feel frightened and alone. That's okay. Like clouds across the Sun, I have faith that even when I don't have faith – even when I can't see the light – the Buddha is still there, smiling at me.

Colin is a long term Sangha member and Lay Order member living in Newcastle.

It was back in 1994 that I first encountered Buddhism. This is when I joined the Amida Trust training programme. Although this early encounter with Buddhism was mainly from a Zen perspective, I now realise that Honen and 'his' Pure Land were very much in evidence.

Pureland Buddhism felt like a more accessible form of Buddhism than others. For me it was a clearer way to get in touch with the Buddha's teaching.

What I like about Pureland Buddhism is that it is a link to the Buddha's heart.

When day to day life's experiences get a tad too difficult, holding the Buddha in mind can help alleviate the stresses.

My practice is mainly recitation of Namo Amida Bu. Although I do also have a shrine room where I read from the Amida *Nien Fo Book*. This helps to create a positive environment for me. By doing so this helps me to feel a closer connection to Amida and also to the wider community.

Namo Amida Bu.

Mindfulness
Kaspalita

Mindfulness is in vogue. Yesterday someone sent me an article on how a short course of mindfulness practice can help businesses. You can take degree courses in mindfulness at some universities, and some mindfulness based therapies are available on the NHS.

If we take the term mindfulness to mean a practice aimed at creating a particular state of mind, as it is often taken these days, then what kind of mind are we looking for, and how can that help us?

In *Not Everything is Impermanent* and *Buddhism is a Religion* Dharmavidya has questioned whether this 'state of mind' is the true meaning of mindfulness, but in this section I'll be using the term as it is commonly taken.

Mindfulness practice is about the observation of how things really are, both in the world and inside our own hearts and minds. To do this most effectively we need a mind with some steadiness – it's no good being distracted all the time, or being side tracked when we encounter something a little difficult. We need a mind that is awake and alert rather than lethargic, and we need a mind that's relaxed.

We rarely, if ever, achieve this state of mind perfectly. A couple of hundred years ago, in South East Asia, monks and nuns would have been asked to practise creating a focussed mind for up to ten years before moving on to other practices. I imagine they were better at concentrating after those ten years than they were before, but we can put even a small amount of relaxed concentration to good use.

The basic mindfulness practice that is taught in the West is watching the breath. We do this by sitting in a formal meditation posture, and then by bringing our attention to the breath – noticing all of its different qualities. If we become distracted or lost in thought, as soon as we realise our attention has wandered we return to the breath.

Doing this practice daily allows our busy minds to settle a little, and teaches us concentration and patience. It trains us in cultivating a relaxed and alert state of mind.

Some people stick with this practice for their whole lives, and whilst it's possible that this practice on its own can lead to insight and compassion, there are two dangers.

The first is that we use the practice for the kind of repression I talked about earlier: to help us keep whatever we have stuffed into our long bags where it is, rather than dealing with it.

The second danger is that it leads to a state of quietude. This quiet passive state can be lovely, and is worth enjoying if it arises in your meditation practice, but don't let it stop you going back out into the world and taking action.

In the Satipatthana Sutta, the text which many mindfulness courses and practices are based upon, the Buddha begins by explaining how we should pay attention to the breath, but he doesn't stop there. He goes on to talk about how we should pay attention to our bodies, how we should fold our clothes (or robes, as he was talking to monks) with care and attention, how we should wash our food bowls and finally how we should be mindful of the Four Noble Truths.

There is a clear movement here from mindfulness of ourselves to mindfulness of how we are in the world, and from the small ways we take care of our environment to the Four Noble Truths, which describe the redirection of our energy to the holy life.

The Buddha was not interested in quietude for its own sake – he wanted us to develop the capacity of being at ease with ourselves and others so that we could love more deeply, so that we could live inspired by a vision of a better world, and act in compassionate ways.

I think breathing meditation is a great thing to have as part of your spiritual practice: it allows the mind to settle and for more relaxed and aware states of mind to appear. This in itself is a good thing, as it can allow us to be more at ease in the world and less driven by compulsive thoughts.

However, from a Pureland point of view, there are two particularly importance places we can direct our mindful awareness.

We can turn our attention to ourselves in a deeply honest way, looking at what's leaking out of our own shadow, and looking at how our behaviour impacts upon others. The nei quan practice, which will be explained later, is ideal for this. It shows us how, in relationship to others, we often take more than we give, and cause harm to others often unknowingly.

We can also turn our attention to Amida and to the Pure Land. The word nembutsu is most often used to mean recitation of the Buddha's name, but the Chinese character nein (or nem in Japanese), refers to memory, contemplation and awareness. Reciting the name is one way into this remembering, but any act of bringing the Buddha to mind is nembutsu.

A world in which we have access to a Buddha is very different to a world in which there aren't any Buddhas. A world without a Buddha is a world without hope – where suffering seems to create more suffering endlessly. A world with a Buddha offers liberation. There is someone that we can go to who accepts and loves us just as we are, and is able to inspire us to perform loving acts ourselves.

It can feel very difficult, even impossible, to take compassionate action if we don't have a space where we are accepted just as we are. What stops us from acting is usually fear, that we will be rejected, perhaps, and this often feels like a survival issue. It probably was once a survival issue: as infants we were dependant on the whims of at least one other person to survive, and historically rejection from the group has often meant death or severe suffering.

In some places rejection from the group can still have devastating consequences, so with all of this in mind we often choose to act in ways which won't rock the boat, rather than following our loving hearts.

Knowing that there is someone we can turn to and feel accepted by can make all the difference and gives us the courage to act in new ways.

Even if we don't always feel intimately connected with the Buddha (and we probably won't) we can remember times when we have done, or times when we have glimpsed the Pure Land, or we can learn to trust the experience of others who have seen these things. Or perhaps we put our trust in the teachings of the Buddha and our experience of practicing them. The Buddha said that whoever sees him sees the Dharma, and whoever sees the Dharma sees the Buddha, so this too can be a kind of nembutsu.

The classic mindfulness practices are helpful for their own sake. They can help us in the short term by producing pools of calm during the day. They can help us in the longer term by teaching us a steady and non-judgmental way of paying attention which we can turn to ourselves or the world. However we wouldn't begin these practices if we hadn't already met the Buddha in some form – if we hadn't already been inspired by something beyond our usual mundane existence. We start from the Buddha (perhaps we meet him through an article on mindfulness in a glossy magazine) and we return to the Buddha. Regardless of what practices we do, and whether we are able to keep doing them or not, what keeps us on the spiritual path and heading towards liberation is our inspiration and our connection with something greater. It is when we forget this that we can start to stray and that is why the most important thing to be mindful of is what we take refuge in: Amida Buddha, Buddha Shakyamuni, the Dharma, the Sangha and the Pure Land.

What do I have to believe?
Satyavani

For most of my life I'd always felt a bit rebellious as soon as I had heard words like dogma, belief or religion. I didn't like being told what to believe, or the idea that anyone could know anything for certain.

As I committed more deeply to Buddhism, and was encouraged to consider it further, I could see that we all already live by certain dogmas – without which we wouldn't get very far. Dogmas such as 'gravity exists' or 'to love others is a good thing to do' give us short cuts in our daily life so we don't have to worry about floating up to the ceiling in between here and the door, or get confused about whether we should hug our friend hello or steal their money.

My initial approach to the dogmas of our school of Pureland Buddhism was to put them aside and not worry about them too much while I gained experience of the practice and started taking refuge in the Sangha. As time has gone on I've been able to test the three dogmas against my experience. Do they seem to describe what happens? Are they a helpful way of describing spiritual experience? So far the answer is a tentative 'yes'.

We only have three dogmas in Amida-shu Buddhism. They are like the essence that remains when you boil everything else away.

We start where we should always start, with the Buddha. The first dogma describes the threefold nature of the Buddha. This threefold nature is known as *trikaya nature* – tri is Sanskrit for three and kaya means body or manifestation. These three ways in which the Buddha is present, or three 'bodies', are known as Dharmakaya (the presentation which embodies the principle of enlightenment and is formless, limitless, and inconceivable), Sambhogakaya (the aspect of the Buddha that we meet in meditations or visions) and Nirmanakaya (an actual incarnated body which manifests in time and space). Dharmakaya is also known as the truth body, Sambhogakaya is also known as the bliss or enjoyment body, and Nirmanakaya is also known as the transformation body. Learning these three terms is the quickest way to sound clever as a Pureland Buddhist!

In Pureland Buddhism, a Sambhogakaya Buddha is also seen as those Buddhas who began as bodhisattvas and became Buddhas because they completed their vows. Amida Buddha is therefore seen as a Sambhogakaya Buddha when the word is used in this way.

This first doctrine, trikaya nature, both provides us with a way of thinking about the Buddha – asserting that he is a spiritual phenomena as well as a person-in-the-world – and also gives us a vocabulary for describing spiritual experience.

It is said to be impossible for human beings to have a direct experience of Dharmakaya (although we may intuit the existence of this realm) as it's just too far away from our own finite plane of existence. I have heard Dharmavidya use the analogy of electricity – we can't make use of 'raw' electricity fresh from the power station (Dharmakaya) or it would blow us up. We need it to travel along cables and to go through several transformers before it becomes something manageable – something that powers our kettles, televisions and washing machines (Sambhogakaya). In this way the Buddha's immeasurable power is filtered or transformed into experiences we can all catch glimpses of – deep gratitude, blissful or transcendent experiences during meditation, a feeling of being connected to everything, a difficult-to-describe awe that moves us to tears when we look out across the sweeping valley or hear a blackbird singing or circumambulate the shrine room and catch sight of the Buddha's smiling eyes following us.

The second dogma brings human beings into the picture. It states that we are all foolish beings of wayward passion. This foolishness is known as 'bombu nature' and Kaspa has written about it in his chapter above. You might think we don't need to be reminded of this, but it is important in Pureland Buddhism to take a realistic view of our capabilities and limitations, and this dogma is here to remind us not to get carried away in feeling we are masters of our own fate. As I continue to investigate this in my own life, I can see how my behaviour is often driven by self-serving motivations operating at deeper and ever more subtle levels of consciousness, often covered up with layers of self-deception which paints a much more flattering picture of why I've taken action.

For example I always feel pleased when new people come to our Buddhist services and I would like to see this as 'me selflessly wanting to spread the Dharma'. This is definitely a part of why I feel pleasure, but I am also driven by needing to see myself as 'a good priest' and needing other people to see me as a good priest too. If lots of people come then I can prop up the part of my ego that needs this affirmation from others. This isn't about what is good for them but about what is good for me. In my experience, it's always helpful to assume that we usually have a mix of selfless and selfish motivations for everything we do and to uncover as many of these selfish motivations as we can, getting them 'onto the table' where they become less harmful to other people.

The bombu paradigm gives us permission to do this because it states that, if we are human, we will be moved by all kinds of selfish impulses that we are more or less conscious of – like a piece of cork in a stormy ocean. This is our starting position. This doesn't mean that we don't have free will (although Jodo-Shinshu Buddhists, the biggest Pureland school, may take a different position on this) but that our free will is more compromised than we imagine it to be. My own thinking is that we are always capable of making the decision which leads to more good – the ethical choice, the selfless choice – but as a result of these powerful ego-driven currents this might be an extremely difficult (sometimes *almost* impossible) thing to do in practice. We are heavily conditioned not just by one lifetime of karma (the way our parents brought us up, the ways we developed defenses to keep ourselves safe, etc.) but by many many lifetimes (the way our parent's parents treated them, the way society has been shaped over thousands of years, etc.).

I have found a great deal of relief in this dogma. It gives me permission to be just as I am – I don't have to pretend any more, or feel that I am different to anyone else. It also begins to point me towards the third dogma, which is that as a fallible human being I can call out for help from something bigger-than-me.

The third dogma is the primacy of nembutsu among Buddhist practices. This dogma selects one Buddhist practice as the most suitable practice for foolish beings such as ourselves: calling out to Amida Buddha and allowing his grace to soak into us. We have written more about the nembutsu elsewhere.

So here are our three dogmas. The Buddha exists. We are fallible beings. We can be saved by saying the name of Amida Buddha. What do we do with them? And what happens if we don't agree with them? Here's what the provisions of Amida-shu say:

> These three [dogmas] constitute the core teachings of Amida-shu. Different members of Amida-shu may interpret these teachings in different ways. Amida-shu is in favour of personal spirituality and regards these three teachings as a framework within which individuals pursue their spiritual quest. The nature of faith, the real meaning of a 'spiritual Buddha', the value of particular practices, and so on are things for the practitioner to find out through experiential immersion, experiment, and reflection. Amida-shu is thus a school of Buddhism with much scope for enquiry and is not a 'hand-me-down' set of dogmas, even though it does provide a simple frame within which enquiry can proceed.[7]

My own experience of the dogmas is that they help me to remember that amongst all the different things we do

---

[7] *Amida Shu Provisions for Structure, Continuity & Governance* (2014)

as Pureland Buddhists – the ceremonies, the practices, the various Sangha activities – what is central is that we are foolish beings, the Buddhas are wise and compassionate, and we can reach out to the Buddhas and be influenced by them by saying 'Namo Amida Bu'. Pureland Buddhism can sometimes seem like a complicated religion, but this is what it all boils down to – say the name, don't worry too much about the rest, and everything will be okay. Even when it's not okay, it will be okay.

I'll leave you with a longer quote by Dharmavidya:

We say that there are three fundamental teachings in Amida-shu:

> The threefold nature of Buddha
> The twofold nature of the practicer
> The singular nature of the practice.

The Buddha is the object of refuge and source of grace in three ways: as absolute truth [Dharmakaya], as spiritual presence [Sambhogakaya] and as physical manifestation [Nirmanakaya].

The practicer is 'bombu' in being fallible and vulnerable.

The practice is singular in that nembutsu encompasses all.

Taking refuge in Buddha we choose the nembutsu as our single practice and, when we have done so, all practice becomes nembutsu.

We take refuge because we realise that we are fallible and vulnerable and incapable of saving ourselves from spiritual danger by our own power unaided.

We are able to take refuge because we attain faith by perceiving with our own senses, by having that faith enhanced by spiritual realisation, and by grounding it upon the intuition of absolute truth that lies beyond our immediate comprehension.

This summary encompasses the whole doctrinal and practice basis of Pureland.

Namo Amida Bu.[8]

---

[8] Brazier, David *Three Fundamentals* March 22 2009 http://amidatrust.ning.com/profiles/blogs/three-fundamentals

Thank you, thank you, thank you

Satyavani

> Most human beings have an almost infinite capacity
> for taking things for granted.[9]

Aldous Huxley

When I first became a Pureland Buddhist, and was still
finding my way with what felt like a strange practice, I had a
Skype session with my mentor, Padma. He told me that when
we say, 'Namo Amida Bu' we are saying it not as we might
say, 'please' – wanting something that we haven't got. We are
saying it as, 'thank you' – and acknowledging how we are
already supported in a myriad of ways. I also heard
Dharmavidya say something like, 'All the Buddhist practice
we do is a demonstration of our gratitude to the Buddhas.'

At the time I wasn't really clear about what I was
saying thank you for. I'd been doing the practice without
thinking too hard about it, but I didn't really feel like I'd
received anything. I guess I had some kind of enlightenment
experiences in mind – a blissful feeling of an intensity I'd
never known, or a sense of profound calm. I was still waiting.

---

[9] Huxley, Aldous *Themes and Variations* (1950) Ayer Co
Pub

Looking back, I don't think Padma was suggesting that I say thank you for my yet-to-be-experienced spiritual experiences. He was suggesting that I say thank you for: the roof over my head, parents who spent many years wiping my nose and clothing me and feeding me and loving me, my education, the radiators keeping me warm in my house, the vets for saving my cat Tsuki's life, the sunshine on my face, the delicious sandwich I'd just eaten for lunch, the invention of light bulbs, the encouragement I received from other writers when I was just starting out, the difficult experiences which have taught me something I probably couldn't have learnt any other way and which made me who I am, this computer, this candle....

Right now I am being supported by the ground and kept tethered to my chair by gravity. I am here and I am me because of the chain of my ancestors going back and back into the mists of time, and because of the very specific combination of DNA that was created when my mother's egg was fertilised. I am kept alive by the correct mix of gases – by this breath, going in and out of my body twelve times every minute. When I pause and examine how much I have received and am receiving in every moment, I am staggered. It is miraculous.

This is the gratitude that my teachers were talking about. And it is very easy for most of us to forget about these things most of the time. Instead we are preoccupied by the things we haven't got, or the things we want to push away. My throat is a little sore today. I woke up late and so I'm rushing to get some writing done before my first client arrives. We've run out of my favourite tea bags. Woe is me....

I also think we tend to avoid feeling grateful as gratitude reminds us of something we'd rather not be reminded of – our utter dependence on a myriad of conditions, and our lack of control over a good many of those conditions. We're not in control of whether the sun shines on us, whether we will be made redundant, whether our children will fall ill, or even whether we will still be alive tomorrow. Acknowledging our dependence on so many conditions beyond our control might make us feel vulnerable and maybe even a bit frightened. Can we trust that our children will get well? Can we trust that we will survive even if we are made redundant? Can we even know that the sun will keep on shining?

Of course, bad things do happen. As we will see later, the inevitability of discomfort and suffering is the first of the Four Noble Truths which the Buddha taught again and again. When you are in the midst of deep grief or pain it might sound insulting or even cruel to suggest that things would improve if you just 'felt more grateful'.

I have found that even when I'm up to my neck in difficulty, feeling grateful can help me to put things in a broader perspective. I am still breathing. The plants are still offering me oxygen. Just now, a friend brought me a cup of tea. I am not alone, even if I feel like I am. Things are better than they were five years ago. Maybe in another five years I might look back on this as the event that finally turned my life around – that forced change and that changed everything for the better. Whatever is true, and whichever small things we can find to say thank you for, say thank you.

One of the annoying phenomena of life is that we are generally less likely to receive the things we're desperately seeking. Think of someone urgently seeking a new partner, or someone selling their car who needs to repay a debt that afternoon. These 'needy' vibes end up pushing away the very things we want to attract. If we practise gratitude, we will feel more secure with what we already have, and we approach these transactions in a very different way. We are more likely to be interested in our dates, rather than thinking about what we can get from them or trying to get them to like us. We can wait until the right person comes along to buy the car – someone who will pay a good price and be pleased with the purchase.

Connecting with gratitude is an excellent way for us to weaken the power of our greed, hate and delusion (our fear). It also strengthens our ability to be present to what we are being offered (our faith). But what can we do if we're just not feeling it? I know people who weren't shown any examples of how to be grateful as they were growing up (except instructions on how they *ought* to be grateful, which isn't the same thing at all). When those around us think, 'the world is out to get you', or, 'other people always get a better deal', these beliefs sink into our marrow, becoming pervasive and deep-set, and getting in the way of gratitude. It can take some time to re-train ourselves to open up to seeing how much we do receive and to feeling thankful. Here are some suggestions for how you can experiment with gently strengthening your own gratitude muscles:

1. Start a daily gratitude practice. Buy a beautiful notebook and make a commitment to writing down a list of five things you've felt grateful for at the end of every day. They can be little or big – the end of a cold and being able to breathe again, a particularly delicious apple, your neighbour smiling at you.
2. Say thank you. When someone gives you something (a cup of tea, a bit of advice, their time) make sure

you take time to receive the gift. Appreciate it, and if you can't appreciate the gift (maybe a Christmas jumper?) appreciate the intention behind the giving. When you can feel the gratitude, say thank you and mean it.

3. Be curious about your habits. What is getting in the way of gratitude for you? Is it a tendency to compare yourself with people who are receiving more which leads to you feeling hard done by? Is it too much busyness? Is it that you feel you don't deserve to receive anything? Be curious about what happens when you write your gratitude list or say thank you. You might want to do some journalling or speak with a friend to explore your attitude.

4. Fake it to make it. It can be helpful to imagine that we are saying thank you, even when (especially when) we don't mean it. Don't do this because you 'should' but because you are interested in what it feels like. In the twelve-step programmes they say 'fake it to make it', which means acting as if something is true and trusting that the genuine feeling will catch up with you sooner or later. You can see how this works when you manoeuvre your cheek muscles into the shape of a smile – hold them there for a while and you might start to feel the flicker of a happy feeling.

5. Do ten minutes of nei quan every day. You can read how to do this in the section on spiritual practices.

One more story, which my teacher told me after he had attended a talk by Ando Sensei, a teacher from Japan. Ando Sensei is a Shin Buddhist (the biggest school of Pureland

Buddhism) and he gave a lecture on Shin Buddhism which was extensive and very detailed. At the end of this very long talk he said that the whole thing could be summarised as 'Thank you very much!' Gratitude is at the heart of Pureland Buddhism, and at the centre of any spiritual practice that helps us to see our place in things and enjoy the wonderful gifts that we are receiving all the time. Mountains. Muesli. The wisdom of our ancestors. Ladybirds. Aeroplanes. Hand cream. Laughter. We haven't earnt them. We don't deserve them. And yet – here they all are. We can practise accepting these gifts graciously, really enjoying them, and allowing the warm glow of gratitude to radiate out of us.

Sujatin is Head of the Amida-shu Ministry Team and has recently moved to Perth in Scotland where she has started a local group.

I came from a background of nearly three decades of practice in an eastern meditation technique based on teachings from the Vedas, with associated study in Ayurveda and Vedic science. In 1998 I found myself attracted to Sogyal Rinpoche's *The Tibetan Book of Living and Dying*. I discovered that a friend was leading a weekly study group in Wigan, about 5 miles away from where I lived. She was a student of Dharmavidya and she invited him to visit and lead an evening event where he gave a talk based on the teachings in his book, *The Feeling Buddha*. I was tremendously moved by his talk and, indeed, felt in retrospect that the Buddha had grabbed me. Life was never to be the same. I began studying with Dharmavidya from this point. So I guess that rather than finding Pureland Buddhism, it was Pureland Buddhism that found me.

I had very little experience of any forms of Buddhism having only studied Sogyal Rinpoche's book for about four weeks before meeting Dharmavidya. Shortly after beginning the other form of meditation in the early 70s I had had a thought that I should be a Buddhist, but I never followed this up as there were no Buddhists in the vicinity and I was tied up with two small children and studying to be a teacher so I continued with my other practice quite happily.

What I like about Pureland Buddhism is to know that I am loved and accepted unconditionally by Amida. And that, although I can possibly make some improvements to myself through my own effort (although even this is debatable), it is Amida who saves me, who has already saved me, irrespective of my faults, feeble efforts, or deserving power. That my practice is not in order to gain anything thereby but comes from my profound gratitude for all that I have already received and continually receive – immeasurably more than I could ever deserve even if I were a faultless person – which I will never be. And that, even as imperfect as I am and will continue to be, I can offer this understanding to others.

Buddhism and my Buddhist practice helps me in my life by helping me experience that I do not need to 'knee-jerk react' to my experiences. Also, it ameliorates the tendency to judge myself harshly and to judge others (which tends to be less harsh). This is because, as I come to accept that I am foolish, yet still loved and accepted as I am, so I am more accepting of others' frailty and foibles. As I allow myself to see more clearly that, even with the best will in the world, I fail, I am affected by both inner and outer forces and conditions, those that I am conscious and unconscious of, so I can accept that this is the human condition and all others must be similar.

In terms of practice, most days I chant Nembutsu and sit in meditation for periods of up to 90 minutes. I chant out loud or silently while cooking, gardening, walking. I spend time looking at my garden, watching the birds and other wildlife and looking at the distant mountains. I listen to music.

The practices of Nei Quan and Chih Quan help me to have a realistic and modest opinion of myself. They also help to make me aware of the enormity of what I receive – immeasurably more than I could ever achieve myself or deserve. I also become aware, through attention on that which is 'not me', of how awe-inspiring and marvellous the natural world, the whole universe, is. I have become increasingly grateful for people, creatures and the natural world. This feeling of awe and gratitude is delightful to experience.

The four sights
Kaspalita

There is a story about the Buddha, and about what compelled him to lead the holy life, that is almost like a legend. We're not sure if it really happened as it's told in the story, or even if it happened at all, but it contains a great teaching and talks about universal experiences and I think this is why it has resonated down the ages.

It is a story about the Buddha called Siddhartha Gautama, or Shakyamuni, who lived and died in northern India and Nepal 2500 years ago and who started the Buddhist tradition.

When he was born his father, a king, called upon various fortune tellers to predict the life of the infant prince. Three of them said that he would become a great king or a great sage, but the fourth said that the young prince would become definitely become a great spiritual leader. As he said this he became sad, as he foresaw that he himself would die before Shakyamuni attained enlightenment.

The King, Suddhodana, wanted his son to become a king rather than a spiritual teacher, so he surrounded his son with all the pleasures of the royal court, and the greatest political and martial teachers.

The story says that the Buddha led a cosseted life – the troubles of the world were kept from him. He lived his life in the summer palace in the summer and in the winter palace in the winter. He travelled between them in beautiful carriages, avoiding encountering the real world.

Siddhartha's mother had died during childbirth, and I can't help imagining what effect this would have had on the King's attitude to his son. Perhaps the King really did become an overprotective father.

So the young prince was brought up in an environment with both of these energies: that he should learn to become a great king, and that he should be protected from all the woes of life.

By the time the prince was 29 years old, he had a wife and an infant son, but felt dissatisfied with his life. He decided to venture out of his protected environment and into the world for the first time. He took a chariot, and asked his charioteer to take him out of the palace.

Whenever I think of this story, I imagine them heading to a local marketplace. I'm not sure if it mentions this in the sources or if it's my own embellishment. If I put myself in Siddhartha's shoes I'd want to be taken to where I could see all different kinds of life, and when I think of my own visits to India, it's the marketplaces that come to mind. Whilst he was out he saw four things which changed the course of his life.

The first thing which set the young prince thinking was an old man. Legend has it that he had never encountered an old person before – the king didn't want Siddhartha to worry about aging and so kept him surrounded by young beautiful people. Siddhartha asked his charioteer what had happened to the man, and the charioteer explained it was simply what happened to all of us: ageing.

They journeyed on and soon encountered a sick person. Siddhartha had the same kind of experience again.

Whenever people in the palace had fallen sick they had either been treated quickly and recovered or whisked away. Here was someone who was really ill and the sight impacted upon the prince. His charioteer explained that everyone gets sick sometimes.

I had met sick people, of course, before I travelled to India for the first time, but the physical suffering of some of the people I saw begging at the side of the road was arresting and thought provoking and this was the kind of intense encounter that Siddhartha had.

Next on his journey he saw a dead body. I imagine this was a funeral procession, carrying the body to the charnel grounds, or it may have been a dead body laid out at the charnel grounds, ready for burning, or perhaps just a body at the side of the road. Whichever it was, it brought home an existential truth to Siddhartha: we are all going to die.

Seeing these three things, the old man, the sick person and the dead body left Siddhartha troubled and thoughtful. How could he find peace in a world full of such suffering?

With this troubled mind, he continued on his journey, and soon Siddhartha saw the fourth sight: a holy man.

The holy man, an ascetic who had devoted himself to the spiritual path, looked at peace in the world. He looked untroubled by the suffering around him and unswayed by the busyness of life. There was something about him that inspired Siddhartha – he saw that it was possible to be in this world with its old age, sickness and death and to have peace in your heart.

As a Pureland Buddhist I find this moment of inspiration crucial to the story: right at the beginning of the

Buddha's spiritual journey it is not through his own calculation that he sets off on his spiritual quest, but through meeting a holy being.

This is how we move from *samsara* to nirvana. We meet the trouble of the world and long to find some way for things to be different. In that moment of despair we can't imagine a way out of suffering. Somehow we need to trust that it is possible to be in the world in a different way. For Siddhartha the idea of salvation or enlightenment didn't come out of his own meeting with old age, sickness and death, but through meeting someone who had already walked the path. The inspiration for liberation comes from outside us.

I encountered my own 'holy man' in those stories about Zen monks that I read online. A friend of mine remembers a Buddhist monk visiting her school when she was young. We meet the idea of liberation in different places.

This encounter is what gives us faith that rather than being simply bogged down in suffering, a different way of being is possible.

In the course of one lifetime we will meet many instances of sickness, old age and death, and many other things which have the potential to trouble us, to leave us feeling deadened and without hope.

We will also meet inspiration – in real people, in stories about people, in the natural world, in the experience we have in guided meditations, or through spontaneous spiritual experiences.

As a Pureland Buddhist we can think of this as Amida appearing to us in many different ways. You might prefer to think of it as many different Buddhas reaching out to you. The spirit of nembutsu is to be grateful for these moments when they arise, to keep remembering that we have experienced them, and to remember that liberation is possible.

After seeing the holy man, Siddhartha went home with a great deal to think about. That night his father had organised a party with lots of dancing girls. They all danced into the night and perhaps being surrounded by beautiful young women distracted Siddhartha from his thoughts. As the party wound down, people began to fall asleep. Siddhartha woke in the early hours of the morning, and looked around him and saw the girls in various states of disarray. In that moment he saw them for what they really were, not a beautiful fantasy, but people who were also subject to sickness, old age and death. In that moment he remembered the holy man and made the decision to leave the palace and his princely life behind, and to seek a spiritual teacher.

The inevitability of suffering: Four Noble Truths

Satyavani

Just now I walked along the long corridor to my office in the temple, passing the open doors of the living room and the library. A small dark lump caught my eye on the library carpet. I looked closer.

It was the top half a mouse; his eyes were open a slit as if he was just sleepy. His intestines spilled from the truncated corpse and a small dark red organ lay a little distance away.

I cleared up the mess and came into my office to write.

Suffering is all around us. Kaspa and I both follow a vegan diet, and we are careful that our cleaning products and toiletries don't contribute to animal suffering. We feed the birds and donate money to animal charities. Our three cats lead very blessed lives, living amongst many people who love to stroke them.

And yet. We kill worms and small creatures when we dig the soil for our vegetable patch. We sit on the leather sofas which came with the house and so we rest on the skins of animals, killed long ago. We bring in packets and packets of meat for our cats. We strike matches which are made using gelatin (made by boiling skin, tendons, ligaments, and/or bones) and isinglass (a substance obtained from the dried swim-bladders of fish).

It is a good thing to try and avoid causing suffering to other beings. This is what Buddhism is all about. But if we begin to think that we can escape suffering entirely, then we are mistaken.

It was suffering that inspired Shakyamuni to ultimately leave the palace where he was closeted and indulged by his father the king, and venture out into the world. It was suffering that led him to his first experience of *samadhi* (a state of peaceful concentration, or consummate vision) when he was a young boy, after his sadness at the worms cut in two during a ploughing festival led him to sit under a rose-apple tree and sink into contemplation.

After he became enlightened, the very first teaching the Buddha gave was a teaching about suffering. He repeated it many times over the next thirty five years as one of the most fundamental of all his teachings – the Four Noble Truths.

In this chapter I will draw on Dharmavidya's interpretation of the Noble Truths which differs from that of other teachers – and shows us a very human side of Shakyamuni Buddha. I'd recommend that you read the whole story in his book, *The Feeling Buddha*.

The first Noble Truth is: *dukkha*. Suffering exists. The word dukkha is commonly translated as suffering but it can also be translated as affliction, unsatisfactoriness, irritation, attraction or aversion. Dukkha is what happens when we want something we haven't got, when we don't want something we have got, or when we are confused or cut off from experiencing an object. Dukkha happens when we encounter impermanence, and it is the physical and mental suffering that arises from birth, illness, old age and death. It is the truncated mouse. Dharmavidya also talks about dukkha as when we are in 'spiritual danger', with the danger being that we might close down, lose faith, lose our bearings or cease to follow the noble path. The events listed as dukkha are not all inherently painful (for example, some people have good deaths if they are completely relaxed), but they are moments that often inspire greedy, hateful or deluded reactions. It's not so much that suffering exists, but that things exist which we usually react to in ways which cause suffering.

The second Noble Truth is: *samudaya*. When we encounter suffering, a reaction to this suffering rises up in us. I see the mouse and I feel repelled, and sad, and guilty.

The third Noble Truth is: *nirodha*. It is possible to harness the power of this reaction and use it for the good of all beings. I decide to use the energy of this reaction in my writing, to help me try and explain the Four Noble Truths.

The fourth Noble Truth is: *marga*. If we are able to do this, we will naturally live a life described by the 'Eightfold Path' – Right View, Right Thought, Right Speech, Right Action, Right Livelihood, Right Effort, Right Mindfulness and Right Samadhi.

Some interpretations of the Four Noble Truths hold that our aim is to eliminate suffering by cutting our attachment to anything that would lead us to suffering – if we can root out the feeling of attachment to the mouse, then we won't feel sad when we see it.

Instead, Dharmavidya maintains that the Buddha called these truths 'noble', and so his intention wasn't that we try to avoid suffering altogether.

He says:

> The Buddha is saying that to be a human being who necessarily suffers is a dignified thing to be. What he is overthrowing is the idea that the spiritual quest consists of a flight from suffering. On the contrary, it is the flight which is undignified and shameful.[10]

Thus the Buddha is telling us that although we can't avoid suffering, we can live a noble life and face difficulty head on, avoiding the temptation to cling to the things we desire, push away the things we don't want, or shut ourselves off in denial or ignorance. We can harness the energy that is released through bumping into things and tripping up, and channel it into doing more good.

I'll give you an example. Last week I had a meltdown.

A few weeks ago I read a story in Amanda Palmer's book, *The Art of Asking*. It's about a farmer who is hanging out on his porch. A friend walks up to say hello and hears a terrible yelping and squealing coming from inside the house. He asks his friend what the awful sound is. His friend says, 'Oh, it's my dog – he's sitting on a nail.' The friend says, 'Why doesn't he just get off it?' and the farmer thinks for a while and says 'Doesn't hurt enough yet.'[11]

Our habit patterns are very deeply entrenched. They were formed when we were very small, and they think that they are protecting us from something terrible – from death. Therefore as human beings we continue doing the things that cause us pain, often for a very long time. One of my habit

[10] Brazier, David *The Feeling Buddha* (2001) Robinson
[11] Palmer, Amanda *The Art of Asking* (2014) Grand Central Publishing

patterns is that I take on too much and I don't ask for help, and I soldier on getting extraordinary amounts done until I suddenly feel alone and overwhelmed and broken.

As I melted down last week, I felt angry at myself for getting myself into that state *again*. But it also felt different. The depth of the dukkha led me to a clarity that I hadn't felt before. I knew I needed to change my approach to the world. I needed to surrender.

I don't think I'm cured. But I did feel enough pain that day to honestly reach out to several people, to put some new processes in place, and to renegotiate some of my responsibilities. I funnelled the dukkha into doing some things that would help me (and others). I finally got up off the nail.

I find the Four Noble Truths helpful in several ways. They reassure me that I'm not doing something wrong if I'm suffering – I'm just having the same experience as the Buddha, and as the rest of the human race. They help me to make sense of the process of forming habits: we experience strong reactions to dukkha and (when we don't successfully channel the energy into a good place) we handle this by pulling something else towards us, running away, or blocking the experience with denial. It shows me how an ethical life is a natural consequence of making the noble choice when we experience suffering. It also connects me to the Buddha. He taught these truths because this discontent is what drives people, and he knew that because he'd been there too. He taught the Four Noble Truths because he wanted to help us. He has helped me.

Honen
Kaspalita

No introduction to Pureland Buddhism would be complete without mentioning Honen Shonin. Honen was a Japanese Buddhist monk who lived in the 12th Century, selected nembutsu as the essential practice, and founded a new school of Buddhism.

In Honen's Japan, enlightenment was the preserve of a small group of people. The best that everyone else could hope for was rebirth as one of that small group of people in their next lifetime. But most people thought that rebirth as one of that group was unlikely, and worried about what they thought was their more likely rebirth in hell or in one of the animal realms. Even rebirth as a human may not have been appealing: during Honen's lifetime there were several famines, natural disasters such as a great fire that swept through the capital city in 1177, and plenty of civil unrest.

Who was that small group of people for whom enlightenment was a possibility? Just Buddhist monks. Nuns were excluded, the best they could hope for was rebirth as a man next time around. Not just anyone could be a monk, the emperor had taken to signing off the lists of ordinands, which meant that to become a monk you had to come from the right sort of family and have the emperor's favour. In the stratified class culture of Japan this excluded another huge swathe of people.

This was the world that Honen was born into: feudal, full of uncertainty and with limited chance of salvation. He was born in 1133, and when he was nine years old his father was killed, probably assassinated as part of a political feud. Legend has it that Honen's father's last words were, 'Don't hate the enemy but become a monk and pray for me and for your deliverance.'

Honen went to live and train in an uncle's monastery, and eventually went on to Mount Hiei, the centre of Buddhist learning in Japan.

When Honen was eighteen he withdrew to a *bessho*, a place devoted to religious practice away from the more worldly affairs of temple life. There was a lot of corruption within traditional Buddhism at that time – the selection criteria for promoting monks had become relaxed and family connections had become more important than conduct. Some modern scholars take Honen's move as a criticism of the life he had found in the temples, as well as a move towards a deepening religious practice. There were several besshos on Mount Hiei and the one Honen moved to was famous for nembutsu recitation.

At that time, nembutsu practice was understood to be just one of the many ways practitioners could accumulate merit, rather than the essential practice Honen later framed it as.

Honen was seeking the deep peace that his father had instructed him to find, both for himself and for the people he saw suffering around him. The Buddhist practices he was exposed to were all about getting better in order to secure a good rebirth and then, ultimately, enlightenment. The trouble was that when he looked deep into his own heart, despite his reputation as a wise scholar and a monk who diligently kept the precepts, he could see plenty of greed, hate and delusion. If he saw this in his own heart, he thought, how could ordinary people whose livelihoods and passions drove them to break the precepts hope for salvation?

Perhaps he was disheartened, or perhaps seeing this stirred compassion in him. Either way, legend has it that he read through all of the texts in the library many times looking for something that would guide him to peace.

A few words in an old Chinese commentary on the Contemplation Sutra spoke to him. These few words, by Shan Tao, were like a door opening for Honen, letting light into a dark room.

Shan Tao said, 'Simply bear in mind wholeheartedly the name of Amida whether walking, standing, sitting or lying down; whether one has practised a long time or short; never abandon this name from one moment. This act brings rebirth in the Pure Land, it is in accord with Amida Buddha's vow.'[12]

As described in the *Larger Pure Land Sutra*, Amida Buddha had vowed to bring all beings to the Pure Land regardless of how much merit they had or have; simply call the Buddha's name wholeheartedly and despite your wayward passions, you will be brought to salvation.

Honen felt the truth of this deep within his own heart. He felt loved and accepted by Amida Buddha and knew that Amida Buddha would love and accept all beings, and bring them to salvation, if they called out to him using the nembutsu.

_____

[12] *Honen's Religious Conversion* accessed 2/11/2015 http://www.jsri.jp/English/Honen/LIFE/conversion.html

This was not a practice of measuring oneself against some ideals, and working towards that ideal. It was not a practice of pulling oneself up by one's own bootstraps to enlightenment. It was simply allowing enlightenment (in the form of Amida) to grasp you and lift you into the Pure Land.

Honen looked into his own heart, the heart of a renowned monk, and he saw that it must be enlightenment, or Amida, or nirvana, or the Pure Land – something measureless – that grasped him, and not the other way around. How could it be otherwise when his own heart was full of karmic seeds and stubborn passions? There was something that was not him that could love and accept him just as he was, and this was his great liberation.

Dharmavidya writes that, 'Spirituality is a progressive learning about one's humanity. When I look back on fifty years of spiritual training what I see is not so much progress in morality as progress in a certain kind of wisdom and by this I do not mean that I have become more God-like, but rather the reverse. The wisdom that seems to have been really important and that I am most grateful for has been the progressive – or rather, by fits and starts – arrival of a sense of my own limitations, fallibility, proneness to short-term temptations, and so on.'[13]

This is the same kind of wisdom that Honen had. He was humbled by his own experience, and reading Shan Tao's words allowed him to intuit and to feel deeply the presence of Amida Buddha.

---

[13] Brazier, David *Not Everything is Impermanent* (2013) Woodsmoke Press

Honen was 43 when this happened. He left Mount Hiei and moved into Kyoto itself, spending the rest of his lifetime teaching nembutsu practice to monks, nuns and to lay people from all different backgrounds, from farmers to samurai warriors and from politicians to geishas.

He established the first Pureland school of Buddhism, teaching that nembutsu was the only practice you needed to find rebirth in the Pure Land. Other practices were good, he said, but they couldn't guarantee a good rebirth, because we are simply too wayward. Only grace can save us from ourselves.

This is the deep intuition that lies at the heart of Pureland Buddhism. It is this that is transmitted from teacher to disciple, and it is this that awakens us when we look deeply into our own hearts.

Anthony is a long-time Zen student and a member of our group in Malvern.

I found Pureland Buddhism by chance when we moved to Malvern. I found many differences in Pureland compared to my previous tradition, Zen. There was a lack of formal sitting meditation. Initially nembutsu practice seemed like an easy option. Also I was a bit bothered by bombu nature which seemed to come across as a little flippant and jokey rather than as a fundamental of the Pureland teaching. As time went on the relaxed approach to the teachings with little dogma helped me to develop a deeper feeling for Pureland and some understanding. I also find the Malvern Pureland Sangha to be more interpersonal and more open than any Sangha that I have previously been involved with.

Buddhism has helped me come to terms with certain difficult aspects of my very early days. Hopefully now there is less ego, I am less judgemental and easier with other people (I need to ask others about this!) As an old man with many years Zen training my at home practice remains silent, sitting zazen with some chanting e.g. Refuge, Repentance and Bodhisattva Vows. But Pureland practice has been assimilated into my Zen practice and sits very happily with it. Whether zazen or nembutsu I am sure that my practice in ordinary daily life has benefited from all the teachings and for this I am grateful.

Radical simplicity: the nembutsu
Satyavani

One of the things I really like about Pureland Buddhism is that it is radically simple.

What it says is that: in order to grow in faith and become more loving, all you need to do is one thing. Say the name of Amida Buddha. Say the nembutsu and Amida will take care of everything else.

Pureland teachings have been around since Shakyamuni's time, but, as you've read, Pureland first became a flourishing independent school in Japan in the 12th Century.

The practice was based on a Buddhist text, *The Larger Pure Land Sutra,* in which Shakyamuni Buddha described a king from the distant past, Dharmakara. Dharmakara encountered a Buddha called Lokeshvararaja and was inspired to become a Buddha himself. Dharmakara spontaneously uttered a series of vows including what is known as the 'Primal Vow' – that he would only become a Buddha once everyone who had heard his name, even once, was guaranteed rebirth in his Pureland.

Different people conceptualise the Pureland in different ways. If you're new to Pureland Buddhism you might want to look at it as the 'field of merit' surrounding a Buddha. When we are in the presence of a great person who is wise, peaceful and loving, we have the experience of becoming 'infected' by their spirit and we become more wise, peaceful and loving ourselves. We might also feel more secure and safe – the kind of feeling you get in a crisis when someone is there who you know you can rely on. This feeling might not even be because of the practical ways in which this person might help, but because of their quality of solidity or a settled confidence that helps us to feel more confident ourselves.

In the text, Dharmakara did indeed become a Buddha – Amida Buddha, the Buddha of Infinite Light (*Amitabha* in Sanskrit). As Dharmakara had said that he'd only become a Buddha when all his vows had been fulfilled, the 'Primal Vow' must also have been fulfilled. Anyone who heard (or said) his name could know for sure that they would be reborn in the Pure Land, regardless of what kind of person they were or what kind of lives they'd lived. Amida Buddha is infinitely wise, peaceful and loving, and so his field of merit is very powerful. You can imagine that entering the physical (or metaphysical) space close to him, his Pure Land would both inspire you to become more loving, and also offer you this feeling of settled faith.

As Kaspa wrote, Honen was inspired by Shan Tao. Repeating the name was the single practice that Honen selected as being suitable for ordinary foolish beings such as ourselves. We simply say the name of Amida Buddha, and we don't need to worry about anything else.

Shinran Shonen, who followed in Honen's footsteps and founded Jodo-Shinshu, the biggest school of Pureland Buddhism in Japan today, said: 'This is indeed the true teaching which is easy to practice even for ordinary, inferior people.'[14] How does this kind of simplicity work in practice?

In our experience of running our temple in Malvern in the UK, people don't tend to need the story I've told above in order to enjoy or make sense of the practice. They come along, join in with our Buddhist services, and either something hooks them in and they return, or they don't come back. In practice the things that hook them in are often the welcome they receive from fellow Sangha members, or the peace they feel after spending time in the shrine room, or maybe even the chocolate brownies!

On first impressions it might not seem like our form of Buddhism is simple at all. Our Buddhist services include reading and chanting Buddhist texts, walking meditation, prostrations, and the celebrant making offerings to the shrine. Our Pureland Buddhist heritage is long and complex. Our own particular Sangha, Amida-shu, has a culture with a very particular flavour which includes psychotherapeutic awareness, an emphasis on a realistic approach to our limitations and the three dogmas you've already read about. It can take a while to work out what's going on, never mind whether it's the kind of place you'd want to spend more time.

Our Sangha is a diverse bunch. We have people from a wide range of economic and educational backgrounds, of different ages, different capabilities and with very different histories. We have people with a long history of spiritual practice and experience, and those who never imagined they would ever become Buddhist. Some of our group have successful careers and healthy relationships, whilst others

---

[14] Shinran Tr Inagaki, Hisao *Kyogyoshinsho* (2003) BDK & Numata Center

have had worse luck with their karma and daily life is a struggle. All have at least had a glimpse of the message of Pureland Buddhism – connect with Amida Buddha and you will know that you are acceptable, just as you are.

You could say that the spirit of welcome that infects new Sangha members is also the nembutsu – it is the way we tend to relate to each other when we feel the security of being held by Amida Buddha. As people continue to practise the nembutsu they find themselves being transformed – feeling less afraid, trusting more, opening their hearts. They come into a closer relationship with Amida Buddha and his good qualities rub off on them. This is the beginning of faith.

It is a simple practice for foolish beings. Thank goodness. Foolish beings just like me.

Being a Bodhisattva

Kaspalita

The Bodhisattva vows:

> Innumerable are sentient beings
> *we vow to save them all*
> Inexhaustible are deluded passions
> *we vow to transform them all*
> Immeasurable are the Dharma teachings
> *we vow to master them all*
> Infinite is the Buddha's way
> *we vow to fulfil it completely*[15]

The Amida School of Buddhism supports and champions the *bodhisattva* ideal. A Bodhisattva is a being who puts working for the spiritual benefit of all beings at the centre of their own life. Bodhisattva activity is any action which brings other beings towards liberation.

As well as thinking of our own bodhisattva activity, we can also reflect upon the ideal bodhisattvas, like Quan Shi Yin, who embodies compassion; Manjushri, who can cut through delusion or Ksitigarbha, who made a vow to keep returning to the hell realms in order to save everybody there.

---

[15] *Nien Fo Book: The Service Book of the Amida Order* (2015)

These are enlightened beings who have promised to return to the world lifetime after lifetime until all become enlightened.

The word bodhisattva is Sanskrit and it means awakened being. Bodhi has the same root as the word Buddha, and means awake. Sattva means person. What is it that we awaken to? There are many different spiritual teachings that the Buddha gave; karma, the Four Noble Truths, and so on, and each time we see the truth of these and put them to work in our own lives we are having an awakening, but the most important thing for a Pureland Buddhist to awaken to is the saving grace of Amida Buddha, and our own bombu nature. We awaken to the fact that there are Buddhas in the Universe, and we are grateful for this.

From this gratitude springs compassion for all other beings, and the desire to bring them to the same kind of awakening. As we experience the joy of faith we long for others to feel this too: we long for others to awaken to the Buddha's love. To the degree that we have this feeling and act upon it we are bodhisattvas ourselves.

When I joined the Amida Sangha I found it difficult to trust people, and I found it hard to believe that I could be accepted just as I was. The Sangha is not made up of Buddhas; there have been times when I have antagonised people and had people be upset with me, and there will be again, but generally I have felt held and accepted in a way which I don't often experience elsewhere.

The Sangha, at its best, is a reflection of the Buddha, if a little bombu at times. The more time I spent in and around the Amida Sangha, particularly in those early days when I was living in The Buddhist House, the more I began to trust that I could be loved just as I was.

I am sure that I would not have been able to have the successful marriage I do have if I had not spent those four years living intensely within the Sangha before meeting Satya. What pleases me the most about the temple we're now running in Malvern is that people are able to feel at home here in the same way that I feel at home in the Sangha, that they allow their defences to drop a little, and that they are able to relax and begin to trust that it's okay to bring the whole of themselves here.

It's not particularly fashionable to talk about your spiritual experiences these days, but there have been times in my life that I have been moved to tears by suddenly feeling, in a very deep way, that I am loved by the Buddha. I have had these moments on retreat at my teacher's home in France, and I have felt it deeply in front of a shrine to the Virgin Mary in a London Cathedral, so much so that I fell to my knees in front of the shrine. It's unusual for me to forget myself in such a way, but the sense of love and acceptance, and my own gratitude, was overwhelming.

Although the Virgin Mary is not a Buddhist figure she embodies the Bodhisattva spirit and I felt that very keenly in the Cathedral. She embodies the compassionate ideal. When we experience such a deep feeling of love it is natural to want to share this deep experience of being loved and accepted. But as the old saying goes, you can lead a horse to water....

We live in a world shot through with suffering, and in response we can become disappointed and defensive. We try to love, and it's not received as we hoped, so we learn to love less fully. Or we long to be loved, and if love doesn't come our way when we hope for it we are guarded later on.

We inhabit cultures which are already full of greed and hatred. (Perhaps these places where hatred rules are the hell realms that Ksitigarbha vowed to work in.)

This is the workplace of the Bodhisattva. To the extent that we are awake, that we have felt loved by the Buddhas, and seen through ordinary human delusion, we long to awaken others.

It is not an easy job; sometimes it is heartbreaking. Having to watch people re-creating suffering over and over again is a difficult thing to see. Despite that, bodhisattva work is the most satisfying of work. Perhaps this is because love longs to be shared, perhaps because of the moments when people begin to let go of their own defences and you see their faith deepen, and the love spreads. Perhaps it is because the more we love, and work for love, the more deeply we feel loved (by each other and the Buddhas) in return.

I am thankful for the Buddha's teachings on human nature and karma which help give us some understanding of why we choose to recreate suffering, and for his example in how to live more lovingly alongside that.

The movement I have described above, from the feeling of being loved to wanting to love others or bring others to the Buddha's love, can be thought of as the inside-out working of the Bodhisattva ideal – from the stirring of our heart to action in the world.

We can also relate to the Bodhisattva ideal in an outside-in way: examining our actions and how we are in the world in relation to this ideal, and allowing ourselves to be moved at what we discover.

In our services we recite the Bodhisattva vows, quoted at the top of this chapter. The essence of these vows is that we make a commitment to liberate all beings, and vow to be reborn as many times as it takes in order to do so.

This is a huge aspiration and it sets up a tension between the bodhisattva ideal, the innumerable number of sentient beings, and our bombu nature.

How can we possibly save all beings from egotism? As Buddhist practitioners we live in the space between the ideal and the actual. We set the best intentions that we can, whilst knowing that sometimes those intentions will be infected with selfishness that we are not even aware of. We know that even with the best intentions our actions can be unskillful, and even skilful actions can be received in all sorts of different ways.

If I only look to the ideal I can end up feeling frustrated. Why are my actions ineffectual? Why do I feel rejected sometimes when I reach out to others? Am I inadequate?

If I keep the ideal in mind, but also look deeply into human nature and into the nature of this world, I find myself feeling tender towards the human condition, both in myself and others.

This tenderness of heart arises when I hear people share their stories in a stone passing, or on retreat, and the more experience I have of this deep listening to people's stories, the more I understand that this is how it is to be human, not just for the people who I am listening to, who are able to make themselves vulnerable and share their troubles with me, but even the people I struggle to relate to.

If I remember that this is how it is to be human when I am in a difficult relationship, or a difficult moment in a relationship, then I can start to find my way to kindness even for the people I find to be hard work.

In this way my own liberation arises alongside the liberation of others. Compassion wells up in me, springing from a deep sense of fellow feeling. In these moments true bodhisattva activity is possible. It is not about me being helpful, or being seen in a particular way, or even about being received well by the other, but a genuine feeling of wanting the best for all beings, and a tenderness in knowing how hard it is for us to escape our karma, and even to take that escape when it is offered.

In December 2013 Susthama Kim, a member of our Sangha, was recognised as an *acharya* (a senior Buddhist teacher). During her ceremony our teacher Dharmavidya talked about how difficult it is to help people, and that often the best way of liberating beings is to simply live your own life in the light of the Buddhas.

Awakening rests on faith, but we cannot force faith into people's hearts. Instead we can live from a place of faith ourselves and allow that to affect how we are in the world. Living from faith, from our own experience of the love of the Buddhas, will naturally move us to that place of tenderness towards others from which genuine compassion flows.

A personal relationship with Amida
Satyavani

As I've said, before I was a Buddhist I poured scorn on religion of all varieties, especially Christianity, the religion I was most exposed to growing up in the UK. As I write this I'm wondering why my feelings were so strong. I think the need for me to feel in control of my life was very powerful, and so any whiff of our dependence, especially on something that I couldn't see or prove and that didn't make any logical sense to me, was seen as a challenge to this self-sufficiency. Why would people need to rely on a spiritual being when they could depend on themselves? We can always take refuge in ourselves and in our ability to control everything around us, can't we?

After I became Buddhist, and as the years have ticked on, I am finding a phenomenon in Christian books that I can't seem to find much of in Buddhist writing, particularly in Buddhist writing by teachers in the West. The Christian writers seem to speak of it quite naturally, as if it is something the reader is taking for granted. This phenomenon is their personal relationship with God.

This personal relationship seems to have many dimensions, which vary for the individual writers. Three of the primary characteristics seem to be a feeling of deep love towards God, a feeling of being loved and looked after in return (and the accompanying feelings of faith, comfort and sometimes bliss), and a willingness to do whatever God asks them to do as an expression of this love and as an acknowledgement that God knows much more than they do and can guide them much more skillfully than they can guide themselves.

Saying the nembutsu and other forms of Buddhist practice help me get closer to Amida: to deepen my relationship with him, open myself up to his grace and help me put my own self-centred ideas aside and make space for something else. As a result, I certainly feel more love and gratitude towards the Buddhas: for all they have given me, and for the refuge I find in the Buddha, Dharma and Sangha. I also have the experience (sometimes in a vague hard-to-put-my-finger-on way, sometimes more strongly) of being loved and cared for by the Buddha. But what about the third characteristic? What does it mean to turn our will over to God or to the Buddha, and to do what God wants us to rather than what we want to do?

Is there a God-like being up in the sky who has a plan for my life? I don't know. Sometimes this idea seems far-fetched and ridiculous to me. How could there be anything that 'knows better' in such a complex world, and how would it have any free time to look after my destiny as opposed to the destiny of countless other billions of people?

At other times, especially when I stop trying to think about it and just immerse myself in this 'way of being', it seems ridiculous to me that it could be any other way. Even if it were just the Earth as a giant organism, regulating itself with a series of complicated manoeuvres – even if it were just the wisdom of everyone I come into contact with – even if it were simply my own subconscious bringing me answers that I can't access when I think of what 'I' should do – I can't quite believe that there isn't a grand benign 'unfolding' which is far beyond the plan my own little brain can come up with.

My sometimes-wavering belief in the benefits of trusting in an unknown-to-me grand plan rather than my own plan has evolved after years of observation and experimentation. To begin with, I watched others who seemed to have a deep connection with spirituality and noticed how they seemed to be different from others. They exuded a kind of deep quiet confidence, and (as I would later make the link) this led them to take more risks with their lives, and to be more courageous in their loving. I saw this most clearly when I joined the twelve-step groups. Rather than becoming weak, those people who were more dependent on their Higher Power seemed to be more 'together' – more whole as people. I began to try this out for myself. When I was overwhelmed I 'handed things over' to the Universe and found some relief. I also discovered that when I could acknowledge that I didn't know the answer to a dilemma and 'asked the Universe' for guidance, the answers that came to me were usually more sophisticated and courageous than the ones I could come up with on my own.

If 'letting Amida decide' is a concept you're not familiar with (or if it sends shivers of cynical incredulity through you!) I'll say a little more about how it works for me. If I am feeling stuck about something then I will make a decision to 'hand it over' to Amida in my mind and let him work it out. It may be that I need to make a big decision about whether to continue a project, or I might feel overwhelmed by feelings of frustration with someone without really knowing why. This 'handing over' usually gives me some immediate relief for two reasons. The first is that in handing it over I've acknowledged that I'm not handling it very well myself – admitting that I'm not after all the Master of the Universe and that some things are beyond me is always a good thing for me to do! (It's actually quite a relief not to be Master of the Universe.) The second reason is that once I've handed it over I'm not on my own with it any more – Amida is helping me. If it's a big and gnarly problem, I might have to hand it over again and again as it returns to haunt me in the small hours of the night or as I worry away at it, playing out the same scenarios endlessly. After I've handed it over I will then patiently keep my ears and eyes open for anything that pertains to my problem. Answers might come to me through something that someone else says, or a thought that arises from nowhere, or something I read in a book. It might be that the answer comes more directly, as I sit with the Buddha and have a surprising new insight or even hear the voice of the Buddha telling me what to do.

It's worth saying at this point that the solution to the problem may not come immediately, or in anything like the time scale you had in mind! When I was in a floundering relationship and didn't know whether I should stay or go, I was advised to stay in the relationship, keep looking at my own part in the difficulties, keep handing the dilemma over to my Higher Power and just wait. It was a year of waiting (and attending a twelve-step programme) before the solution came to me, and when it came it was crystal clear. I hadn't been ready to hear the solution earlier in the year. It would have been much harder to live that year 'not knowing' if I didn't believe that there was some kind of bigger plan which I didn't understand just yet. This year of not knowing and working on myself was a year of much change, during which I learnt lessons which have proved crucial to me ever since.

How do we know that the solutions that come to us are 'God's will and not mine'? This is a big question, but here are a few suggestions. Amida's solutions will come from a place of more love and less fear. They might present themselves to us persistently, for example, three different people might give us the same advice that is counter to the direction we're currently heading. Sometimes on hearing the solution we might feel a (sometimes reluctant!) knowing in our stomachs that this is what we have to do. Another characteristic is that the solutions do seem to take us further than we would go on our own – the insights are from outside our own ego structures. One of my twelve-step sponsors would say that God's plan for her was way grander and more magnificent than she could ever have imagined for herself. From a Buddhist perspective we would say that Dharma or truth is things-as-they-are, and that we can only truly see things-as-they-are if we are looking through eyes unclouded by ego. The only way we can do this is with help from outside – God will intervene to whip away the veil from our eyes.

The biggest example of this working in my life is the one I gave earlier about running a temple full of residents, the last thing I thought I ever wanted to do. Amida knew better! Another characteristic of the solutions that come from God is that we can trust that we will only be given what we can handle – like Jesus said, his yoke is light[16].

And so my personal relationship with Amida means that I trust him to know best, that I feel love towards Amida, and that I feel Amida's love towards me. Not just a blanket, cover-all love, but a very specific love towards Satya, as Amida knows me better than I know myself. Being loved is

---

[16] Matthew 11:30

my favourite part about being a Buddhist, and the most unexpected. I feel like I'm in a relationship with something that never lets me down, that loves me unconditionally, and that is always there for me. I feel the glow of this love and I know that it exists underneath everything else, supporting me and giving me courage.

If this isn't within your own experience then it may sound pretty odd, as it would have sounded to me a decade ago. That's okay – take what you like and leave the rest. But if you are intrigued and maybe even want a taste of this yourself, what can you do to get closer to your own Higher Power?

There are a million different answers to this question – as each of us will find our way in our own unique fashion. In fact, rather than thinking about it as finding your way, think of it as being led, and of allowing yourself to be led.

Look for clues in the Universe. Are you drawn to attend a particular class, read a spiritual book or spend time in a church? Do you want to get to know someone spiritual better? Are you interested in the idea of having a small shrine in your bedroom, or going for walks in nature and practicing gratitude? How might you approach your Higher Power – by saying please (praying) or thank you? By handing your problems over? By putting yourself in her hands, even if you don't know what that means or how you might carry it out? Maybe a phrase jumps out at you when you read the *Summary of Faith and Practice* or you see a quote from St Francis of Assisi on social media. Write it down. Repeat it. See what happens.

Nobody can tell us how (or whether) our relationship with God will develop and deepen. We wouldn't dream of suggesting to our single friends how they might want to kiss a man we think they'd be suited to, or squeeze them both into a hug when they don't even know each other's names. What we can do is spend time with those people who've journeyed before us and see what rubs off on us. We can put aside any defensiveness or cynicism that arises, just for now, and see it as a playful experiment. And we can trust Amida, especially when we feel resistant to doing that and our egos are kicking in with a vengeance. Letting go into God can be terrifying – we are surrendering everything that we think keeps us safe: our self-sufficiency, our control, our identities, our self-centred empires – but it is also the most delicious thing I have ever tasted. I'd love for you to get a taste too.

Sanghamitra is an ordained priest based in King's Heath near Birmingham. He runs an Amida-shu group who meet once a month for practice and study and currently edits the Running Tide, Amida-shu's magazine.

My brother, Kaspa, moved into the Buddhist House in Narborough, Leicester in 2006. I would often ring him and ask if he was free that weekend for a visit only to be told there was a retreat taking place. Eventually, I decided I might as well just attend a retreat. The retreat I was due to attend was based on Dharmavidya's book *The Feeling Buddha*. I didn't know very much about Buddhism at the time, so I thought I'd better read the book before I arrived so I didn't look completely clueless. As I read, I found that the ideas made a lot of sense to me. I had read about the Four Noble Truths before, but I couldn't really make sense of them. Dharmavidya's teaching was rational enough not to be too uncomfortable to my sceptical, scientific mind. I remember there was a phrase that particularly touched me at the time about 'being in the waiting room of life.' It summed up a lot of my feelings at the time.

During the weekend of the retreat, my thoughts about the book and Dharmavidya's teaching were confirmed and I found myself agreeing with a lot of what was said. I very much enjoyed meeting the other people who lived at the Buddhist House at the time, and getting a flavour of what went on there. When I returned home that weekend I decided to become a vegetarian.

Subsequently, I went to visit my brother in Amida France (as it was then) and to take part in his Drama Workshop. By the time I returned the next summer, I felt ready to ask to take refuge.

I had previously been to a nearby WBO (now Triratna) Buddhist centre when Kaspa first moved to Narborough to try and get some idea of what he was doing, but I didn't feel compelled to go back. I also read part of Thich Nhat Hanh's book *The Heart of the Buddha's Teaching*. I found it very difficult to get my head around the idea of stopping suffering by removing attachment. I don't think I actually got all the way to the end of it. Dharmavidya's teaching was a lot closer to how I already saw the world and was much easier to fit into my world-view. It's probably just as well I didn't read *Buddhism Is a Religion* first!

The idea that everyone is accepted by Amida is massively important to me. It's probably a life's work to actually believe it though. Also, the Bombu paradigm gives me permission to be more forgiving towards myself. In Amida particularly, I found David and Caroline's psychotherapy background very reassuring and I have met many interesting people and good friends.

For practice, I chant one or two malas of Nembutsu every day before I go to bed, and I have recently made a shrine in my living room.

How does Buddhism help me? I try to reflect the acceptance I (sometimes) feel out into the world.

Deep listening
Kaspalita

I have learnt a great deal from deep listening: from listening to other people and from listening to the call of Amida.

Here in the Amida-shu community we value listening to each other so much that we make special formal spaces for it. These are known as 'gatherings' or 'stone passings'. Here in Amida Mandala we also call them 'listening circles'.

We sit in a circle and take turns to speak. We use a stone to signify which person is speaking and being listened to, passing it around the group until each person has been heard.

When I first moved into the community in Leicestershire I was very nervous of these meetings. We would meet as a household once a week for a stone passing, and sometimes the training community (those of us in the community who were ordained, or on the road to ordination) would meet separately as well.

One evening, not long after I had moved in, stands out in my memory. We had finished our Sunday afternoon service, we had eaten dinner, and the washing up had been done. I went to the bathroom at the top of the house. The bathroom was nestled under the eaves of the house and had a sloped ceiling. It was around 7pm. I heard the bell ring downstairs to summon us to the gathering. I leant my head against the sloped ceiling and took a deep breath. As the bell rang nervousness shot through me. I didn't want to go downstairs.

What was I worried about? I was thinking more about the speaking and being heard than the act of listening. I was worried that if I shared honestly and people started to see me for who I really was they would reject me, and I was worried that I didn't know myself that well either, and perhaps if I started to share honestly I wouldn't like what I heard.

I did go to the meeting. I would like to say that I went out of a sense of it being a good thing to do, but I suspect it's equally true that I thought that if I didn't go someone would ask me why, and to admit that I was nervous would have left me feeling more vulnerable than going to the meeting.

As I learnt to speak in stone passings in those early days people listened, and most of the time they listened without judgement. If there were reactions from people that worried me, they were held in the larger container of the group. No single person embodies complete love and acceptance all of the time, but the whole of the Sangha is greater than the sum of its parts. My experience of the group was that it was accepting and without judgement.

Not only did I begin to feel comfortable in these groups, I also began to look forward to them. When I spoke they gave me an experience of being accepted just as I was, and when I listened I learnt about the conditions of others' lives. The more deeply I understood their lives, the easier it was and is to love them.

Now I understand that these meetings are holy spaces. The Sangha at its best is a reflection of the Buddha, and coming together in this way can facilitate a deep experience of relationship with the Sangha as Buddha. More often than not there is a great teaching in the words of someone else. It is not unusual that what someone shares from their heart speaks directly to a question I have been holding. Perhaps someone talks about a difficult relationship with a friend, and I learn something about my own friendships, or someone shares about coming to terms with grief, and some of my own grief finds solace.

Looking back on my first experiences of these kinds of groups, I wish someone had told me how powerful it is to listen to other people, and not just how profound it feels to be heard. A great deal of my initial nervousness about this practice came from thinking of the moment when I would have to speak, so much so that I probably wasn't really listening to what others were sharing. If I had been able to give all of my attention to listening, I'm sure I would have felt a lot less nervous. The more deeply we pay attention to the other, the less energy is left over for worry and self-consciousness.

It's possible someone did mention this at the time of course, and I just wasn't listening.

We can listen to each other deeply, we can listen to the Sangha as the voice of the Buddha, and we can practise listening directly to the Buddha.

We can listen to the Buddha as he speaks directly to our heart and we can listen to the words of the Buddha through recorded teachings.

There are many texts which record what Buddha Shakyamuni said and taught during his lifetime, and just a few which mention Amida Buddha, but all Buddhas act and teach with the same spirit.

There's a great deal of wisdom in the teachings of Shakyamuni: advice on meditations, suggestions on how to live a good life, as well as psychological and spiritual teachings. Through reading and studying these, and the commentaries of later Buddhist teachers, we can get a sense of the character of the Buddhas and what they stand for.

If we want the same kind of happiness and freedom the Buddhas have then we should get to know them in this way.

Sometimes when we encounter the Buddha in this form something in the teaching will speak to us directly. It will reach out across time and space and answer a question we have been asking or show us some guidance that we didn't even know we were looking for. If I read a teaching more than once something different might speak to me each time I read the text.

Sometimes when I pray I get an answer. I don't pray for a winning lottery ticket, or any kind of intervention in the material world (although sometimes things happen which feel like grace) but for wisdom and guidance and for faith.

I might sit in front of a shrine, perhaps I'll make an offering, or perhaps I'll just sit quietly and turn my mind to the Buddha. The experience is like tuning in. The dial is usually set to 'Kaspa' and I need to turn it to 'Amida'.

I have done this when I've become stuck in relationships with friends, and I often do this before giving a talk, particularly if I'm nervous.

What I'm talking about is a form of nembutsu, but rather than just reciting the Buddha's name in order to orient myself to the Buddha, there is some specific guidance or support that I am looking for.

I suppose you might call it a deep intuition, or the best part of my unconscious mind at work, but sometimes the answer that comes back is so far outside of what I know, or usually think, that I am sure it comes from outside me.

The felt sense is like this: something that is not me is present and either gives a specific answer or just brings a warm loving presence.

Sometimes I know what the answer will be before I ask, and I think in these cases what I am really asking for is faith and courage to do the right thing, or to be accepted even if I cannot do the right thing. Having a felt sense of the Buddha being near assures me that all will be well.

You might ask, how do I know it's the Buddha and not a more wayward spirit (or if you prefer, a part of me that is more like the Buddha, or more like Mara, the Buddha's foe)? This is where understanding the character of the Buddha is important.

I have met the Buddha not only through feeling his presence in my practice and prayers, but through the records of his teachings. I know the Buddha kept the precepts, so if I am advised to break the precepts, it's probably not the Buddha speaking to me.

It's also true that the more I get to know the selfish parts of myself the easier it is to tell the difference between what I want and what the Buddha wants. Does an impulse feel selfish and self-protective or compassionate? I remember Dharmavidya once saying that we either take refuge in the Buddha, or in our own neuroses.

Sometimes when I pray to the Buddha I don't ask the Buddha for help, instead I ask 'What can I do for the Buddha?'

When I am asking for help there is usually some selfishness involved. Perhaps I am asking for help with good dharmic work, but if I am asking for help what I am essentially asking for is for things to be a little bit easier. Sometimes asking the Buddha for help moves me away from selfishness; it's usually some kind of fear that makes work more difficult, and if I do feel helped there is less fear and therefore less selfishness, and then it's genuinely easier to do the good work. Sometimes asking for help in this way keeps me in a selfish frame of mind: I want things to be easier, but the depth of my karma, and the nature of what I'm attempting means that this job is just going to be difficult. If I've asked for help and it still feels like hard work I can sometimes end up feeling resentful rather than supported. If I ask the Buddha what I can do for him I find that it undermines that selfish tendency.

I am not asking the Buddha to make life easier for me, but to direct me to the activity that is most likely to bring liberation for myself and others. This connects me with a bigger story than the one I usually inhabit, which is about serving my own ends, and it asks me to step up for a bigger cause. Difficulty becomes something to be met wholeheartedly rather than avoided. This is why I feel that my own liberation rests on the liberation of others – it is by going into the world to perform the Buddha's work that I become free myself.

When I ask in this way, sometimes I am directed towards work that takes me out of my comfort zone, and sometimes I am directed to work that is restorative. Sometimes the former becomes the latter when it is held in the Buddha's light.

We hide from the truth in order to keep ourselves safe (or at least that's what our ego believes). Deep listening, to each other, ourselves and the Buddha, brings us closer to what is true and the real safety of liberation.

Safe spaces
Satyavani

Last night I sat in a circle with four people I'm close to and lied to them.

As Kaspa has described, every Sunday evening in the temple we sit in a circle and pass a stone, taking turns to speak and be listened to.

These kinds of spaces are incredibly rare. I'm always amazed at how the stone produces a kind of magic. The words we speak (whatever they are) take on a preciousness as the others all listen quietly. The words of others become tender and wise. The space between us fills up with empathy – we can really begin to understand what it's like for others at the circle to live their lives. (Much like it is for us to live ours.)

I usually come away from the circle feeling warm and fuzzy. Last night I came away feeling resentful and tired. When I had the stone I talked lightly about my week and what I was doing tomorrow.

My lies were lies of omission. What I should have said was: I really didn't want to come along to the listening circle tonight. I'm tired of people. I'm grumpy. I don't want to listen to anyone. Now leave me alone.

I don't know what would have happened next if I'd started with that. I might have felt more angry. I might have cried. I might have realised what the grumpiness was about. But I think it probably would have brought me closer to the people I was sitting with, rather than distancing me further.

> Our society is so fragmented, our family lives so sundered by physical and emotional distance, our friendships so sporadic, our intimacies so 'in-between' things and often so utilitarian, that there are few places where we can feel truly safe.[17]

Safe spaces are scarce for most of us. Even when we find them, it's not easy to make use of them. It's not always appropriate to share what's in our heart, and often we are too afraid to show others what's really going on. I didn't share more honestly because I was scared – of being rejected, of hurting others. That's okay – that's how it was last night.

But if you can look again and find somewhere safe, you will find the magic. I can feel it now. The magic that arises in the circle is a warm and accepting tenderness. Namo Amida Bu. Where are your safe spaces? How can you find more of them?

---

[17] Nouwen, Henri J. M. *Life of the Beloved* (2002) Better Yourself Books

Grace
Satyavani

> I do not understand the mystery of grace – only that it meets us where we are and does not leave us where it found us.[18]

Anne Lamott

As I researched this chapter on grace, I got tangled up in theory. Who am I to say anything about grace? Is there even such a thing? How can I prove it or convince you? Does it always come through divine intervention? How does that fit with the theology of Pureland Buddhism? What would the scholars say?

I don't know what the scholars would say. All I can do is tell you how I use the concept of grace in my own life, and why it is as helpful to me as the knife that spreads jam on my toast.

Grace is the label I give a phenomenon where something from outside of me gets inside me, often despite me, and which points me towards beauty, goodness and wisdom.

---

[18] Lamott, Anne *Traveling Mercies: Some Thoughts on Faith* (2000) Anchor Books

An example might help. When on retreat in France recently I was sitting in the shrine room during morning service and feeling very alone. I asked for some sign from Amida that he was there – imagining that when he appeared he would fill me from my toes upwards with a warm cosy feeling. Nothing happened. Later, on a long walk in the burning midday sun across a flat landscape with no shady relief, just as I was running out of energy, a large tree came into view at the roadside. I stopped underneath it and lifted my face up to a cool breeze that seemed to come from nowhere. The coolness trickled over my face and body, bathing me in deliciousness. I didn't feel alone any more. I felt completely plugged into the divine. I laughed at myself for thinking I should decide when and how Amida would appear, and I felt a welling up of gratitude that so many good things were being offered to me all the time. The tears ran down my cheeks.

Grace isn't always a dramatic event. It may be spotting a tiny Goldcrest with his streak-of-sunshine cap as we wander aimlessly in the garden, consumed with our petty resentments. It may be that as we struggle with a particular relationship we hear a new author's name in several different places, and on buying their book discover exactly what we need to approach the relationship differently. It may be a strange feeling of security or shivers of joy that appear as we step into a Cathedral.

Receiving grace is always a good thing. It always leaves me lighter, less confused or hopeless and more full of faith. In my experience, having the word 'grace' in my vocabulary encourages me to be more open to more of these kinds of things happening again. It helps me to be open to the things I'm not paying attention to, and to broaden the potential field from where grace might come.

Another quality of grace is that it reminds us how much we receive and how little we have done to earn or deserve it. Every day we are provided with oxygen, a place to live, food that has been grown and prepared by strangers, love from our friends and families. If we consider the transport we use to get to work – whether car, bus or bicycle – we can start listing the knowledge and expertise necessary to build the vehicle, the raw materials given to us by the earth, the people who manufactured it, the shop who sold it, the people who paid for and built the roads, the traffic control systems, the emergency services when accidents happen.... Once we start reflecting on the balance of what we receive compared to what we have offered in return we realise that we would never be able to 'pay the world back' for what it has given us.

Acknowledging or even cultivating the feeling that we are undeserving goes against conventional wisdom about what is 'good for us'. We are usually told that we need to 'build up our self-esteem', learn to feel 'entitled to things', and that, as the famous cosmetics tagline goes, we're 'worth it'. In my experience, it is actually when I feel most humble and grateful that I am most able to receive all the good stuff that life has to offer me. I'm not talking about the kind of humility that involves beating ourselves up or punishing ourselves. This is just as much about ego as when we 'puff ourselves up' to feel better about ourselves. I'm talking more about a very realistic appraisal of our conditions and of our bombu nature which leads to a natural sense of contrition. Contrition is the gate through which grace can enter.

So is grace some kind of divine intervention, something we receive from the Buddhas? I don't know. What I do know is that the universe is vast and complex, and is beyond the limits of our imagination. If you laid the axons in your brain end to end they'd travel around the world four times. The sun is 15.6 million degrees Celsius at its core – a piece the size of a pinhead would give off enough heat to kill a person 160 kilometres away. If you put peanut butter under extreme high pressure, you can make diamonds from it. In my work as a therapist, I never fail to be surprised and awed by the inner landscapes of my clients. In a world such as this, anything is possible. Maybe grace is coincidence and wishful thinking, maybe not. It doesn't matter. What matters is whether the concept of grace helps me to keep an open mind and heart, or not. It does. That is enough.

During my research I found a review of a book about grace by Anne Lamott. The reviewer said that Lamott's book was 'a field guide to looking for and recognising the gifts ... that are available to us, whatever our faith, when we open our hearts to that goodness of the universe which is currently beyond us.'[19] I love this description of the process of opening ourselves up to grace. It describes very well the leap of faith which is necessary to allow grace in – something we mostly avoid by making up our minds in advance, deciding whether someone is going to be able to help us or not, and trying to find security by putting up protective barriers rather than

---

[19] Guyette, Angelle *'Small Victories': Anne Lamott writes about grace for those who hate books about grace* Pittsburgh Post-Gazette Dec 21 2014

remaining soft (and vulnerable) and letting the Buddhas help us. I hope that you too might begin to find ways of opening your heart to the goodness of the universe which is currently beyond you. There's an infinite amount just waiting to be invited inside.

Faith in faith

Kaspalita

Dharmavidya has spoken about having faith in faith. I don't want to speak for him, but this little phrase, 'faith in faith', seems to get to the heart of what is transmitted in this form of Pureland Buddhism.

When we think of religions we often think of faith in belief: the world was made like this, or like that; this is how to get to heaven; the spiritual world looks like this; so and so is true, other things are false.

A great deal of this kind of thinking appears to be about making people feel safe, rather than about genuine religious feeling. Human beings prefer certainties to uncertainties: if we know something, we can create a response to it that allow us to keep safe, either physically or psychologically.

It is much harder to keep steady, open hearted, and kind in the face of uncertainties, but this is what faith in faith asks us to do. It asks us to remain open and full of confidence in something we can't quite name in the face of shifting circumstances and suffering.

For me, faith in faith has some of the same feeling as Julian of Norwich's assurance that 'Sin is behoven but all is well and all shall be well and all manner of things shall be well.'

I am suspicious of anyone who claims to know anything completely. We are flawed receptacles of wisdom moving between moments of seeing a little clearly and moments of being in the darkness. I'm aware of the irony in making such an assertion. Nevertheless I do have a sense that a 'faith-full' way of approaching the world is more appropriate and rewarding than an approach in which we look for certainties and sometimes convince ourselves that the certainties are true.

Cordelia was previously a Trustee for the Amida Trust and is based in London.

I found Pureland Buddhism through my teacher, Dharmavidya. I met him and Pureland Buddhism through my original interest in Buddhism in general. I then was lucky to obtain a scholarship to Japan to do research on social work and Buddhism. There I got involved with meditation and then with Pureland Buddhism through the Amida Trust. I was a Trustee (and Chair of the Trustees) of Amida Trust for some years. So I have been involved with Pureland Buddhism for many years!

Pureland Buddhism is very 'open' and I feel it is available for all believers! I feel very touched and moved by the chanting. My Buddhist practice is an integrated part of my life professionally, emotionally and intellectually. I keep the Buddha in mind by trying to meditate regularly and to live an 'aware and good' life. Namo Amida Bu.

The Bodhisattva of compassion
Satyavani

I talked about dukkha in a previous chapter. What else does Pureland Buddhism have to say about suffering?

One of my favourite Buddhist stories is of what happened to Quan Shi Yin (or Avalokiteshvara), the Bodhisattva of Compassion. Quan Shi Yin means 'hearer of the cries of the world', and this Bodhisattva vowed to work tirelessly to help all sentient beings until no-one was suffering any more. Of course, there is a lot of suffering, and legend says that she became so overwhelmed with all this suffering that she shattered into a million pieces. Amida Buddha came to her aid, putting her back together again and enabling her to continue helping. Quan Yin is often pictured with a little red Amida Buddha at her head, symbolising the fact that Amida is always there for her and 'has her back'.

Although we don't notice all the suffering in the world at once, most of us can identify with Quan Yin's sense of being overwhelmed. Sometimes the suffering of others (never mind our own suffering) overwhelms us no matter how hard we try to be good or do the right thing. I take two things from the story. The first is that we need to ask for help, which includes admitting to ourselves that we can't do it on our own. Even Quan Yin, the Bodhisattva of Compassion herself, found it too much to continue with her mission without the support of Amida. If Quan Yin needed help then you can guarantee that this limited human being does! The second is that when we know we are held by a power greater than ourselves we are able to find a new strength and it becomes possible to carry on. This strength or power isn't ours – it belongs to Amida, and it comes through us. It could also be seen as faith – a knowing that we will be okay, that we are looked after, despite all the difficult things that happen in the world. When we have faith, we are more able to step out on a limb, and to experience the inevitable disappointments without losing our conviction.

Most of us don't find it easy to ask for help. In her book *The Art of Asking*, Amanda Palmer says:

> From what I've seen, it isn't so much the act of asking that paralyzes us--it's what lies beneath: the fear of being vulnerable, the fear of rejection, the fear of looking needy or weak. The fear of being seen as a burdensome member of the community instead of a productive one. It points, fundamentally, to our separation from one another.[20]

Maybe this is why Quan Yin waited until after she'd shattered into a million pieces before she asked. I know from my own experience that it seems easier to make myself ill or exhaust myself than it does to say to Kaspa 'I'm overdoing it this week' or 'Can you do the cooking for tomorrow's retreat?'

When we ask for help, we are letting go of the fantasy of infinite self-power, and we are admitting how much we are

---

[20] Palmer, Amanda *The Art of Asking* (2014) Grand Central Publishing

at the mercy of our fallible bodies, our frantic minds and the crashing waves of our emotions. We are acknowledging how dependent we are on a myriad of conditions beyond our control – our own histories, the people around us, the weather, the stock markets.... We are also, as Amanda Palmer says, opening ourselves up to rejection. It's much more comfortable for most of us to be alone without having asked, rather than the awful solitude of having asked and being told 'no'.

On the other hand, asking for help is the beginning of a spiritual life. It is the basis of the twelve-step programmes, which emphasise the extreme difficulty of the first step which is admitting that we can't overcome our addictions on our own. It is outlined in the *Summary of Faith and Practice*: 'Saving grace ... only comes through the sange-mon.' We can receive the grace of Amida only when we have been through the *sange-mon*, literally the 'gate of contrition', where we realise the ways in which we fall short, feel contrite and make ourselves available to be helped. Why would we take refuge in the three jewels if we already felt perfectly secure?

Buddhism doesn't help us to eradicate suffering in our lives or in the lives of others. It is pretty upfront in saying, whatever you do, you will continue to experience discomfort and pain. What it does give us is a broader context in which to contain this suffering, and the encouragement to lean on the Buddha, Dharma and Sangha in order to receive their blessings and continue living our lives as nobly as we can. Maybe there is some ultimate point to all this suffering – maybe there isn't. There is a lot that we don't know. But in the meantime we can remember that Amida is holding us and, if necessary, will put us back together again if we just call out and ask.

The Buddha of measurelessness
Kaspalita

In the Larger Pure Land Sutra, the text which describes Amida creating his Pure Land of Love and Bliss, there is a section which describes the various names of Amida. It says that:

> Amitayus is, therefore, called
> the Buddha of Measureless Light – Amitabha;
> the Buddha of Boundless Light;
> the Buddha of Unimpeded Light;
> the Buddha of Incomparable Light;
> the Buddha of the Light of the Monarch of Fires;
> the Buddha of Pure Light;
> the Buddha of the Light of Joy;
> the Buddha of the Light of Wisdom;
> the Buddha of Continuous Light;
> the Buddha of Inconceivable Light;
> the Buddha of Ineffable Light; and
> the Buddha of Light Outshining the Sun and the Moon[21]

---

[21] Verse 45 *Larger Pure Land Sutra*
http://www.amidatrust.com/amidashu/lpls.html accessed 3/11/15

143

This list gives me some sense of what it is that I am taking refuge in when I take refuge in Amida. Throughout the sutra light is used as a metaphor for love. We still use it that way sometimes in English, someone who is in love is 'all lit up', for example, and a new or expectant mother is 'glowing'. The twelve kinds of light in this list gives us some idea of the quality of love that Amida has for us.

The Buddha's love is measureless. We can take this to mean two different things, each of which describes the love of the Buddha. It is measureless in the sense that it does not measure: we are loved whatever we do and whoever we are. Sometimes a mother will have this kind of deep love for a child, it is unbreakable regardless of what the child does – the child is not measured by the mother. The Buddha's love is also measureless in the sense that it is so vast it cannot be measured itself. Some of the other epithets also point towards this.

The Buddha's love is boundless. It does not stop at the edge of the Pure Land but goes on and on. We draw lines around our conditional human love. We love our family, but exclude others. Or we love our country, but not other countries. The light of the Buddha is not like this, there is nothing you can put between yourself and the Buddha that will stop the Buddha loving you (although we do sometimes refuse to acknowledge the light, when it gets to us). The light of the Buddha is unimpeded.

The Buddha's love is incomparable. It does not compare you to the person next to you and choose who to love or who to love more, and the love itself cannot be compared with anything else. The love of the Buddha is far above and beyond other loves, particularly human loves. When we love another person there are usually all sorts of conditions attached, some conscious, some unconscious. I'll love you as long as you keep loving me, or I'll love you if you agree this is the kind of person I am, or as long as you don't misbehave, or any number of other things. A good relationship moves in the direction of unconditional love, but never gets there and is often more about finding a person whose conditional love is a good fit with whatever your own conditions are. The love of the Buddha is much more reliable than our own.

The Buddha's love is like the monarch of fires. If one great fire is the source of all fire in the world, the flame from which all candles are lit, then we can think of all love as reflections of the Buddha's love. We are able to love to the extent we have felt the Buddha's love (although we may call this love by many different names). The love we feel and encounter in this world is like moonlight, shining clear and bright, but always a reflection of a much greater light.

The love of the Buddha is pure. Our own love has met disappointment, and so is held back or contaminated by fear, or guilt, or anger. The Buddha's love is not affected by disappointment, it keeps on loving, clean and pure.

The Buddha's love is joyful and wise. This describes the kind of love the Buddha has for us. It celebrates our successes and it celebrates us just being who we are – the Buddha's love is always pleased to see us. The Buddha is wise, he (or she) can see the whole of who we really are, even when we cannot. The Buddha knows what is best for us, and longs for it, but loves us whether we can step into that space or not.

The Buddha's love is continuous. It does not stop, whatever we do.

Despite all of the words I have used to describe it, the Buddha's love is inconceivable and ineffable. We make it smaller in order to talk about it. We make it smaller in order to feel it. It is deeper and more vast than the most powerful spiritual experiences suggest.

The light of the Buddha outshines the sun and the moon. These were the brightest lights at the time the sutra was composed, perhaps we can imagine stronger lights now, brighter stars. The Buddha's light outshines these too. And even if we can imagine brighter stars, we cannot even look directly at our own sun without being blinded.

This is what we are taking refuge in when we take refuge in Amida. We talk about calling out to the Buddha, but he/she is right there, we just have to open our eyes.

Modgala is an acharya in the Amida Order and one of the first three Sangha members to be ordained by Dharmavidya in 1997. She has been very involved in social engagement in the UK and abroad. She ran the Sukhavati temple in London for several years and is now a trustee on several Buddhist and interfaith committees. What follows is an extract from her forthcoming book.

Something within me changes as I drive and chant. At first my chanting tails off quite frequently and I have to repeatedly bring myself back to the chant. I am tense and troubled as my longing for my family wars with my quest to live a useful life in worlds alien to those in our well-to-do West. I must write this book on Zambia to bring the plight of the people there suffering from AIDS and many other illnesses and often on the brink of starvation to our attention. Perhaps even more importantly I want to correct people's impression of Africa. In Zambia I found wonderful people, generous in spirit and with much to teach us about living a generous life in harmony with others. I must tell my friends' stories.

My chanting grows more intense. I feel the power of chanting reverberating through me. I feel my heart calling out to the measureless power of Amida to help me wake up from the darkness that threatens me. I feel my mind clearing

– literally my brain is tingling as my resolve to do this work returns.

The dark clouds lift and melt away as I drive and chant. I start to feel the beauty of the world around me again. This is a very physical feeling for me. I can feel the muscles in my body relaxing and can almost taste the brilliant colours around me – azure skies, deep blue lakes and all the colours of gold on the trees that tower beside me. I feel and hear my chanting become more melodic and rhythmic rather than being a dull repetition of the words. It feels like my whole body is singing in the sunlight that pours through the car.

Unshakeable trust

Satyavani

The big golden Buddha on our main shrine holds his hands in front of his heart, crossed over with finger-tips pointing towards their opposite shoulders, palms facing inwards. The Buddha is traditionally depicted with his hands in various positions which symbolise different qualities or actions – these positions are called *mudras*. I looked this mudra up after a nine year old on a school visit to the temple asked me what it meant. It is known as the *vajrapradama mudra* and the fingers can be straight (one palm layered over the other) or intertwined. The vajrapradama mudra is typically translated as the 'Mudra of Unshakable Self Confidence'.

Our self-help society encourages us to spend our time and energy 'building up our self-confidence' – putting work into bolstering our self-esteem and strengthening our sense of 'me as okay'. We are asked to be kind to ourselves and forgive ourselves without question, always giving ourselves the benefit of the doubt.

Being kind to ourselves is a good thing. It is important for us to have a realistic view of how competent and capable we are, which means not undervaluing ourselves or seeing ourselves through the warp of old stories. I also think it's equally important to acknowledge our fallibilities and our foolishness. I don't know about you, but mine runs pretty deep.... How does this fit with self-confidence? Do we

149

have to feel that we are good people in order to feel okay about ourselves?

I've learnt that what really helps me when I'm feeling down on myself or afraid of the world isn't trying to feel better about myself but instead connecting with some sense of 'everything will be alright'. Not alright-perfect, but alright-sometimes-pretty-awful with the proviso that this alright-sometimes-awful is always held in a bigger container.

In one place I found the vajrapradama mudra translated as the 'Mudra of Unshakable Trust'. I like this a lot more. 'Trust' points outside of me, to where the help is. I might not be able to rely on myself as being able to keep everything in control or become perfect, but I can trust in something bigger than me. The Universe, the Buddhas, a Higher Power, God, Humanity. Whatever you want to call it. Faith.

I try not to worry too much about my levels of self-confidence. They come and go. Sometimes I feel smug about the things I've achieved, and sometimes I despair at the depths of my dysfunction and the perniciousness of my compulsions. When I take refuge in something bigger than me and live my life illuminated by this great light, everything else comes out in the wash.

When I'm feeling wobbly, sometimes I try the vajrapradama mudra for a while. You might want to try it too. Hold your hands over your heart. Imagine how deeply you can trust the universe, even if other parts of you are sceptical. Can you feel it yet?

Other power
Satyavani

Most of us like to think that we have control over at least some aspects of our lives. We work hard so we will be promoted, we eat healthily so we won't get ill, and we behave in particular ways around our friends and family so they'll like us, see us in a particular way, do what we want them to do....

Unfortunately, sometimes people are promoted ahead of us regardless of how hard we work. Sometimes we get ill, despite how much we exercise and how healthily we eat. And the people we love (and those we don't love) have a very annoying habit of not doing the things we'd prefer them to do.

Co-dependents Anonymous (CoDA) is a twelve-step programme for people who are co-dependent – people who make themselves safe by trying to control or please others. This group has a lot to offer when it comes to helping us acknowledge the extent of our powerlessness over people, places and things. The first of the twelve steps of CoDA is: 'Admitted we were powerless over others, and that our lives had become unmanageable.' We are all at least a little bit co-dependent. Co-dependency is what happens when we make ourselves into a Higher Power, feeling it's our job to direct or manipulate others for their own good (that is, for our own good) or when we make other people into our Higher Power, relying so completely on their acceptance or approval of us that we'll do whatever it takes to get it. As you can imagine, this causes all kinds of havoc in our lives as we try harder and harder to influence others in various ways.

One example from my own life is how I feel around people who are in chaos. Because of certain events in my life, I can feel unsafe around people who are in denial or acting in chaotic ways. When I encounter people in chaos I do all kinds of things to try and get them to pay attention to their chaos and to start healing it or sorting it out. I might suggest that they seek therapy or encourage them to go to a twelve-step programme. I might point out to them how their actions are affecting others. On the surface it might look like these things are for their benefit (aren't I kind?), but when I make these suggestions more than once and keep making them my other motivations become clearer. I actually need these people to go into therapy for my own benefit, so that they can sort out their chaos and I can feel safer around them, rather than for their own benefit.

Most of our behaviour towards others will contain both selfish (co-dependent) and selfless motivations. Co-dependent behaviour happens because, usually for some historical reason, there is something we are afraid of. We may not have any awareness of this fear at all, but it still drives us to behave in ways that aren't in our best interests or in the best interests of others. Examples are people who stay in abusive relationships because they are afraid of being alone, people who bully others because they are afraid of being vulnerable or 'less than' others, people who are needy and demanding because they are afraid of being rejected....

As with all compulsive behaviour we start in denial about the true impact of our co-dependent behaviour on ourselves and others, because to let go of denial would also mean letting go of the control (which of course we never have to begin with!). To get to the first step, admitting that we are powerless over others, we have to bash up against the consequences of our behaviour repeatedly until it gets painful enough to admit that something isn't working. Some people reach the first step after the break-up of a string of romantic relationships, some after intractable issues with friends, some after realising that they always put up with things that they shouldn't put up with in relationships. Reaching the first step is usually a mixture of anguish, as we face the chaos we've created in our lives for many years and begin to take responsibility for it, and relief, as we let go of some of the denial that takes such a lot of energy to maintain and start to see the naked truth of our situation.

In a similar way, Pureland Buddhism reminds us that we're not as in control as we would like to believe. We are all bombu – foolish beings of wayward passion – and we are blown like long grass in the wind by these often-hidden passions. Our passions (greed, hate and delusion, and the fear behind these impulses) drive us to act in selfish ways, which ultimately cause us trouble. Pureland Buddhism suggests that these passions are too big for us – it is impossible for us to control them. We might try from a position of self-power to curb our greed, by limiting how many glasses of wine we drink or trying not to lose our temper at people, and we can keep some of our passions under control for some of the time, but sooner or later we encounter the deep power of our various compulsions and failings and realise how fruitless it is to believe that we can perfect ourselves if only we try hard enough. We are not only out of control when it comes to our own behaviour and the behaviour of others, but also of material objects, money, the weather, our physical surroundings, and of course how and when we're going to die. This is what the Buddha realised when he experienced the four sights – we're not in control of how quickly we age or when we get sick either. Our only hope is to acknowledge the hopelessness of our situation – our unmanageability – and surrender to the other-power of Amida Buddha. We remind ourselves of how foolish we are every time we say 'Namo Amida Bu' – Namo, little foolish me, calling out to Amida Buddha for salvation.

This is the point at which many Westerners baulk. Other-power approaches are not popular. They strip us of our comfortable illusions of self-control, and ask us to hand ourselves over to something we might not even believe in or understand. Why should I trust this 'Higher Power' more than I trust myself? This reluctance is often compounded by our disappointing or downright damaging experiences of religion when we were growing up, and our experience of being let down by other people and learning that being self-sufficient is the safest way to be. Breaking through all these defences (which were probably very necessary and appropriate when we first developed them in childhood) is why it can take so many painful years to get to the first step – we sometimes have to be very desperate before we acknowledge that we're not doing so well with our own lives and that we might as well give something else a try. As one of my favourite quotes points out, 'This is not your week to run the Universe. Next week is not looking so good either.'[22]

---

[22] Elliott, Susan J. *More on Control*
http://www.gettingpastyourbreakup.com/gettingpastyour past/2007/03/36-tftd-more-on-control/ accessed 3/11/15

Putting ourselves into the care of a Higher Power – Amida Buddha, or however you conceptualise something that is bigger than you and knows better than you – is how we take refuge. We no longer rely on ourselves to know all the answers or to know best, including knowing what is best for ourselves. We open our eyes and ears to the wisdom that the Universe might be offering us. We hand problems over when they are too big or confusing for us, and we wait patiently to be shown a different solution. The solution might come through an insight, through something we read on the internet, or through something one of our friends says when they're talking to us about something else. We develop our relationship with our Higher Power by listening (spending time in quiet meditation or chanting) and speaking to them (making offerings, expressing gratitude or asking for help).

In my experience, once I had released myself (or had been released) from the tyranny of thinking-I-could-control-everything, the relief was huge. Of course, the denial creeps back in. I catch myself trying to manipulate the outcome of a situation, or getting compulsive around the internet. We are foolish beings of wayward passion, after all! We have to take the first step afresh every day, or every time we say Namo Amida Bu. The good news is these mini-realisations of the sneakiness of our egos are the gate through which we experience grace. Amida will find a way to work on us, despite our ego's best attempts to thwart him. We just say Namo Amida Bu and he takes care of the rest.

Karin is an aspirant, on the path to becoming ordained. She lives in Belgium.

From childhood on I was fascinated by the world and interested in meaning. I wondered who I was, what the significance was of living. I spent hours observing the world from behind the window. That image has remained a 'fil rouge' in my life, me and a window and behind that a space in which movement and stillness alternated like low and high tide. Life is a three dimensional plane in which all kinds of different realities are interconnected and interrelated. Chogyam Trungpa Rinpoche once drew a cloud on a white piece of paper, and asked his students what this illustrated. 'A cloud.' they said. 'No,' he answered, 'it is the sky with a cloud in it.' My search has been for that sky, that space that supports and carries everything, that wideness; and for the ability to see the depth and to distinguish them both – the cloud and the sky.

This search has led me along various Buddhist and other spiritual paths. My attraction to Buddhism is that it is a very simple yet profound teaching, which is passed on through a wide variety of schools and forms. I have felt very inspired by interesting teachers with a lot of knowledge, but most of all I developed deep love for some of the practices of the heart, such as metta and mindfulness.

I first encountered Pureland Buddhism when I met David and Caroline Brazier about 15 years ago at a weekend workshop in Belgium. This led to visits to Amida France, the formation of a Sangha in Belgium, and regular retreats with David and Caroline in Belgium. The Sangha still meets today, consisting of Pureland and non-Pureland Buddhists.

I was immediately pulled in by Pureland Buddhism and the teachings by David and Caroline. I felt especially touched by the practice of chanting, by the devotional aspect. I love the foundation of faith and surrender, of opening the heart. The social dimension of other-centredness, of connection and interdependence speaks to me deeply and the call to action with and towards others is so relevant in today's world. I was also attracted by concepts such as our bombu nature – our path is not about becoming 'perfect' but about things as they are.

I am definitely not the best practitioner in terms of 'sitting' or even 'chanting'. I meet in a small Pureland gathering a couple of times a year. I attend a retreat once a year, I create conditions at home that remind me of the Buddha, I practise mindfulness, metta and nei quan in day to day life. And I always wear my mala, it is a great reminder.

Buddhism and my Pureland practice is the foundation of my life, an invisible field that carries me and that I feel connected with. They run as a red thread through my work and life with others. I have the idea that no matter how difficult circumstances are, I will always be supported and I will never be alone.

Spiritual training
Kaspalita

When I first moved into The Buddhist House I was classified as a trainee. There were certain formal things I had to learn before becoming ordained – how to perform certain ceremonies and so on – but being a trainee is also about learning, or taking on board, a certain kind of spirit.

Along the way a spiritual trainee also learns very practical things: how to cater for large groups of people, how to take care of a property and a garden. A spiritual trainee is taken to the edge of their comfort zone for the powerful learning that can happen there.

The spirit is something about faith, something about open handedness, and something about a willingness to do what's best for the community, rather than just for oneself.

We could also talk about spiritual training as Bodhisattva training; it is learning how to love more deeply, and to create the conditions in which others can love more deeply.

When we frame it in this way we can see that a mixture of practical and emotional learning will be part of the process. Love needs to manifest in practical ways in the world, and some of the ways in which we are called to serve love will naturally take us to the edge of our comfort zones, which can bring up all sorts of fears and defences.

Learning how to relate to the emotions that appear in this space is an important part of spiritual or Bodhisattva training.

You don't need to be on the road to ordination to be a spiritual trainee. Buddhism, including Pureland Buddhism, holds that spiritual training is a good thing for everyone to do. Or perhaps we could say that it is inevitable – once we have taken refuge in the Buddha, spiritual training will happen naturally.

As we feel loved and held by the Buddha and the Sangha, some of our defences drop away and our loving heart will want to express itself. We'll take some loving action which will be more or less successful, and our training begins. At some point our compassionate action will fail – either we'll be unskilful, or simply meet a practical limit. In this moment, if we can take refuge again we can experience being held by the Buddha in that difficult moment, and then naturally we'll want to go back into the world and be compassionate again.

One of the first times I was asked to be in charge of the catering for a large group I had a moment of being overwhelmed. I was struggling to imagine how I could produce food for all of these people that were coming. All sorts of defences and thought processes were being triggered. What if I no-one liked what I made? (Or what if just one person didn't like it?) What if I spent too much money? I was exposing myself to being judged and this felt like an extremely dangerous place to be.

Those fears got in the way of me actually taking any steps to prepare and I couldn't imagine what the first step should be.

I knocked on the door of Dharmavidya's office. I could see that he was deep in the midst of work, but he called me in anyway. I nervously laid out my practical problems. The fears about being judged were mostly unconscious back then. He listened and nodded.

I was expecting some practical advice, either some guidance around the cooking, or an approach to take, or even to be sent to someone else who could help.

Dharmavidya said, 'Okay.' He was smiling warmly.

I got the message. This was my problem to solve. I didn't like that message so much at the time. What I saw later, rather than in the moment my troubles were handed back to me, was that Dharmavidya's simple, 'Okay', was an act of faith.

It was an act of faith in my ability to solve this problem myself, and an act of faith in something greater, that even if the food didn't appear when it should have done, or wasn't up to scratch, or I blew the budget for the whole week on take-away food, there would be something greater at work.

Any failure would be held by the Buddha. I could then look at what had happened from a position of feeling loved rather than judged, and learn something not only about catering, but about failure too and the human condition.

The catering went well, no one starved and most people enjoyed the food. Although I'm not sure how they felt about the cauliflower and almond soup that ended up tasting like liquid marzipan.

John Daido Lori said that the teacher's job is to pull the rug from under the spiritual trainee, and then to encourage them and help them to get back up again.[23]

I'm not sure we need to worry too much about pulling the rug from underneath our trainees or each other, life does that often enough anyway. What is important is to keep loving them, and each other, in the way that I was loved in that moment.

[23] Loori, John Daido *Mountain Record of Zen Talks* (1988) Shambhala Publications

A Pureland approach to self-care
Satyavani

There is a particular narrative in Buddhism around an ideal of denying one's own needs and limitations, either in the service of others or as 'spiritual quest'. This narrative has unhelpfully hooked into a part of my own personal psychology which holds that I should always attend to others before I attend to myself. I have started to question this approach (which often leads me to burn-out and to become quite useless to others) and to tentatively find support for my hypothesis in the Buddhist texts.

It was important for me to find a story in the Samyutta Nikaya called the Sedaka Sutta, or the Bamboo Acrobat[24]. In the story, our bamboo acrobat climbs onto his bamboo pole and asks his assistant Medakathalika to come and stand on his shoulders. She does so (I can imagine them precariously balancing) and then he says to her, 'You look after me, dear Medakathalika, and I will look after you – thus with us looking after each other, guarding one another, we'll show off our craft, receive some payment, and safely climb down the bamboo pole.' At this Medakathalika says, 'That will not do at all, Master! You look after yourself, master, and I will look after myself. Thus with each of us looking after ourselves, guarding ourselves, we'll show off our craft,

---

[24] SN 47.19

receive some payment, and safely climb down from the bamboo pole. That's the right way to do it!'

If the bamboo acrobat had indeed focussed too much on Medakathalika, he would have neglected to attend to his own balance and, in falling off the tall pole, would endanger her life. The Buddha is showing us that we have a responsibility to tend to our own balance – whether this be physical, psychological or spiritual – in order to keep ourselves steady. If we are steady, we will be able to support others. This story is the Buddha's version of the instructions you will find on the oxygen masks in aeroplanes – if you need to use them, put on your own mask before you put on your children's.

Of course, sometimes we are required to put our own needs aside and tend to someone else's before our own. If our child is sick and needs to go to hospital, it doesn't matter if we are hungry or exhausted – we do what needs to be done. There are no hard and fast rules in life. Sometimes we need a teaching that helps us to tend more carefully to our own bodies or well-being, and sometimes we need a teaching that encourages us to look beyond our ego in order to let something from outside penetrate the tangled mess.

In the story of the Bamboo Acrobat, the Buddha seems to be encouraging us to become mindful of our own balance using a self-power approach. We notice whether we are off-balance and we then take the appropriate action to put ourselves back in balance. I would see this self-directed awareness of ourselves as only half of the picture. The other half is other-power, and Pureland Buddhism is particularly good at articulating this.

My own experience of Pureland Buddhism is that the nembutsu offers us a powerful experience of becoming more compassionate and loving towards ourselves and others. In every recitation we are acknowledging our foolish selves calling out (Namo) and hearing the response of Amida (Amida Bu) which is to love and accept us, and others, just as we are. The important bit here is that Amida isn't some higher part of ourselves (other Buddhist traditions might conceptualise it as Buddhata or our Buddha-nature) but something that is very much *not* us. This thing that is Not Me takes us outside of our egos. It's impossible to do this ourselves (or maybe practically impossible as it is said that the Pratyekabuddhas became enlightened without the help of any other Buddhas and solely through their own efforts – although there are no Pratyekabuddhas in the Pure Land).

Sometimes we undervalue ourselves as a part of our habitual patterns of behaviour. One of my patterns is to refuse help from others. This comes from my programming which tells me to take care of the other person before I take care of myself. Part of me believes that I can't trust others to look after themselves, and if I don't look after them, they may neglect themselves to the extent that they are then unable to look after me. In this way, attending to them first is a convoluted way of getting my needs met. Recently one of our templemates offered to take some mugs into the kitchen and wash them up. I found myself saying 'no thanks, I'll do them', as I subconsciously attempted to protect him from over-offering and becoming resentful, or burning himself out, or who knows what. I managed to catch myself and took this back, telling him that actually I would very much like him to do the mugs. This allowed him to be an adult and make his own decision and also to do the washing up and feel like a useful part of the household.

I will need to catch myself maybe a few thousand more times (or a few hundred thousand more times) before I completely reprogramme this part of me. Maybe it will never be reprogrammed. And this is where other-power comes in. When we bash up against our limits, whether this is an acknowledgement of our current levels of selfishness or our limits in being able to 'self-improve' this selfishness away, we can feel loved by Amida just the same. This love soaks into us from outside of us and reaches parts of us that we would never be able to reach through our willed efforts. We are putting ourselves into relationship with the infinite – we are not the infinite. When I sit in the shrine room and make an offering of my disturbed thoughts or my disappointment to the Buddha, I am giving these thoughts and feelings away – they are going somewhere outside of me. In return I receive a sense of peace and settled faith that I experience as coming from outside of myself – it is Not Me, and it soaks into me as fine rain gradually soaks the dry earth.

As well as putting others before myself, something else that I hold very strong programming around is in not allowing myself to have limits. This is also a way of keeping myself safe – if I have a limitless capacity to contain others and keep going, then I never need to fear that I will be dependent on others, or that I will fail to meet the needs of others, which would lead to them falling into chaos and threatening my own safety.

Shantideva has some useful advice for me (and maybe you) in this regard, in the following verses from Shantideva's *Way of the Bodhisattva*:

47

First of all I should examine well what is to be done
To see whether I can pursue it or cannot undertake it.
(If I am unable) it is best to leave it,
But once I have started I must not withdraw.

67

When my strength declines, I should leave whatever I
am doing
In order to be able to continue with it later.
Having done something well, I should put it aside
With the wish (to accomplish) what will follow.[25]

Even the Buddha would rest when he was older and
feeling ill – sometimes his attendant Ananda would turn
visitors away in order to preserve his energy. It is permissible
to rest when we need to rest – not just permissible, but
advisable. This is a simple lesson that I need to relearn over
and over, as I catch myself pushing myself beyond my
capacity or feeling terrible about myself when I am no longer
able to contain the emotion of another. I also find Jesus'
words a helpful reminder – 'For my yoke is easy and my
burden is light'[26] If I surrender to Amida's will, I don't have
to do everything for everyone else all the time. I can listen to
my limits and leave what I'm doing, to continue it later. This
is okay!

Where does contrition fit into this picture? Can we
find a way of both nourishing and cherishing ourselves and

---

[25] Shantideva *Guide to the Bodhisattva's Way of Life* Tr.
Gyatso, Kelsang (2002) Tharpa Publications

[26] Matthew 11:30

feeling appropriate contrition when we will, inevitably, get things wrong and cause harm? I think it is helpful to consider how much ego there is in our contrition. The experience of contrition is clean – it burns with the fuel of a deep acknowledgement of our foolish nature, and once we have felt it thoroughly then it leaves no traces behind. We can move on to our next action, which we will approach again with the hope that we will act from pure compassion but the realistic acknowledgement that we will be acting from a mixture of selfish and unselfish motives. If we find ourselves getting into 'beating ourselves up' or compulsively returning to our shortcomings, then it may be that we are making an identity of them and finding some safety or comfort (perverse as this sounds) in being 'the one who always gets it wrong' or 'the one who doesn't measure up to others'. When we discover these props to our ego, we can both have compassion for them from a self-power position, and also expose them to the love of Amida and let them slowly melt away in the warmth.

Pureland Buddhism reminds us that we are starting from a position of fallibility and dependency – as human beings, a lot of what we do is driven by our fear and this includes the ways in which we put ourselves down, distort the worth of the work we do, and act in ways that look like 'taking care of others' but are really 'manipulating others through caretaking in order to feel safer and better about ourselves'. As the love of Amida Buddha shines down on us we can begin to see these patterns for what they are and learn to take care of ourselves with the same loving attention that we offer others and the objects around us. We rub cream into our feet as we would rub cream into the Buddha's feet, and we say no to a request when we are over-committed as we would protect a beloved disciple from driving themselves too hard. As we learn to love the worst parts of ourselves, we find it easier to love these parts in other people. As we learn to love the worst dysfunctions in others, we find it easier to love these dysfunctions in ourselves. Neglecting ourselves and always giving preference to the giving of care to others will lead us to burn out. Neglecting others and always preferring the giving of care to ourselves will cause us to become disconnected from the world and wither as we miss the nourishment of having our love received by others.

Amida, help us to find the middle way, as the Buddha found after he was saved from self-starvation by Sujata the milkmaid. Help us to love others and to love ourselves just the same. Help us to remember, every time we say Namo Amida Bu, that our most hated enemies and the very worst parts of ourselves are loved just as they are.

Trusting
Kaspalita

When we take refuge we put our trust in the Buddha, Dharma, and Sangha. Earlier I talked about living a faith-filled life. These are the same thing: a faith-filled life is a life in which we trust that following the Dharma will lead to the best outcome, or trusting that the Buddha has our best interests at heart without knowing what those best interests are.

We can trust the Buddha and the Dharma completely, but how much can we trust the rest of the world, from the Sangha, made of people at different stages on the path, to people on other spiritual paths? Regardless of where we are in our spiritual journey there are times when we all act from greed, hate and delusion.

Recently some friends of the Sangha came to visit the temple. It was their first visit. A few of us were in the garden working. It was a beautifully sunny afternoon. These friends came down into the garden to spend some time with us. We had cups of tea and cake, and we talked about all sorts of things. On their way out they went through the temple and collected their bags which they'd left in the hallway. A purse had gone missing from one of the bags.

They retraced their steps through the town, calling in at the shops they had stopped in, despite being sure that their purse was in the bag when they arrived at the temple.

The temple door had been on the latch all afternoon. There had been a group using the shrine room, and the shrine room door had been propped open in the afternoon as well. The shrine room is next to the front door and for a while we tried to tell ourselves that no one could have come into the temple through the front door without the people in the shrine room noticing. When the purse didn't turn up anywhere else it began to look likely that it had been taken from the bag when it was in our hallway. Of course someone could have opened the door quietly and slipped in without anyone noticing – the group in the shrine room were concentrating on their own activities, not who was coming and going through the rest of the building.

I was shaken at the idea of someone coming into the temple and helping themselves to something that wasn't theirs. This is my home as well as the temple.

I have always wanted to model trusting people here, from giving people responsibility for different jobs to having a donation bowl that's open rather than a slot into a secure box.

A few years ago something like this might have led me to trust people less, but trusting people has become important to me.

A few days before the theft I'd been reading Amanda Palmer's *The Art of Asking*[27] and she relates a similar story. After years of trusting fans and having that trust rewarded, someone took advantage of that trust in a way that was much more invasive than having a purse taken. She went through a process of questioning how much she should trust people

[27] Palmer, Amanda *The Art of Asking* (2014) Grand Central Publishing

again and then realised that all acts of entrusting (entrusting in samsara, anyway) are a risk. If it's a sure thing we don't really need to trust at all, not in the same way as when we take a chance on someone or something less known.

If we trust ordinary people, sometimes we will be disappointed, and sometimes we will be rewarded. In my experience the more we trust, the more that trust is rewarded. If we go into the world believing that people are generally full of goodwill, we will see and receive much more goodwill than if we enter the world with a suspicious attitude. I don't think that's just confirmation bias – I think people are much more likely to be warm and friendly and willing to help if you are open hearted and think well of them. If you approach someone already believing they are going to rip you off, or let you down somehow, what do you think will happen?

Amanda Palmer decided to keep on trusting people and so did I.

I want to encourage goodwill and open heartedness in the people around me, and if I approach them with suspicion and end up inspiring small mindedness and meanness it doesn't really feel like I'm doing my job properly.

As a Buddhist priest and spiritual teacher, I want the people around me to be the best and most loving they can be, and that means creating the conditions in which that is more likely to happen, not less likely.

Having said that, I make sure there's never more cash than I'm willing to lose in the open donation bowl, and we do keep it inside the temple and not out on the street. Along with being trusted, there's something else which inspires people to be trustworthy: having a relationship with the person doing the trusting.

I'd be surprised if it was someone from the temple community who took the purse. We're much less likely to rip someone off if we have a personal connection with them, if we know who they are, and if we like them. It's not a cast iron guarantee of course, but if we cultivate good relationships, and trust the people we are relating to we're much more likely to have that trust rewarded than if we just leave our purse on a train in the middle of a busy city where we don't know anyone.

Although of course, as Satya will tell you, given her experience of losing her purse on the London underground and getting it back in the same day, there are strangers who are trustworthy too.

I was talking about trusting with Dharmavidya earlier this year. He said that some people have to learn to trust people more (perhaps that's where I'm coming from when I write this chapter – and if you're like me you might find this chapter useful), but that some people have to learn to trust people less. If your early experience of people was that they fulfilled all of your needs and were completely reliable, it can come as a shock to encounter greed, hate and delusion, and the limitations of ordinary human beings. Perhaps if we trust people more than they are trustworthy we can end up supporting their patterns of dysfunction as they take advantage of us.

We can't control whether our trust will be rewarded or not. Sometimes we do nothing and people are kind to us, sometimes we pour all of our energy into a relationship and we get burned. All the same I'm going to keep trusting the people in my community, and looking for the goodwill in strangers.

Our biggest addiction
Satyavani

One way of talking about Buddhist philosophy is as a theory of addiction. We all develop addictions as a way of avoiding the realities of impermanence and loss. We want to hang onto the good stuff, push the bad stuff away and remain ignorant of the stuff that confuses us. As a child we might steal a chocolate biscuit after being told off and as we eat it, we notice that the knot in our stomach feels better. When we feel the knot again, we seek out biscuits. All kinds of compulsive behaviours develop in this way – from the relatively benign (watching television, keeping too busy) to potentially fatal (alcoholism, eating disorders).

We all have our pet addictions, but what is our favourite? When I was ordained my first name changed from Fiona to Satyavani. For the first few months, when people said my new name it was invisible to me. They had to repeat it several times, getting louder, in order to get my attention. Now when someone says 'Satya' I hear it immediately even if the word is nestled in a hubbub of noise. It's like your dog hearing the word 'walkies'!

We notice the same effect when we look at photos of a friend's wedding and find a photo with us in it. Sometimes we may be drawn towards looking at ourselves and admiring ourselves, and other times we may be repelled, thinking we look fat or unattractive. Either way, our selves are very powerful *rupas* for us (a rupa is an object that is highly charged with personal meaning).

This attraction to (or avoidance of) anything related to our own selves goes deep and it makes up the bulk of many of our preoccupations. When we are listening to others we might relate what they're saying to our own lives, and plan what we want to say as soon as they stop talking. We surround ourselves with people, objects and activities that support our identity – wearing clothes that signify 'who we are' to the world and joining various gangs (football team supporters, Buddhist Sanghas....) We love our mobile phones and social media because they often point back towards me, me, me.

Why are we so preoccupied with our selves? Why do we invest so much time and energy in building ourselves up? Before I answer this I want to pose another question....

Is there such a thing as a permanent self to 'build up' anyway? This is where Buddhism messes with our heads! There are various meditations in the Buddhist canon which encourage us to have an experience of the insubstantial and ever-changing nature of our selves. One physical meditation asks us to focus our attention in turn on the gases, liquids and solids entering and leaving our bodies. After many years or even months, how much remains of us that was the same substance as it was before? Another meditation instructs us to imagine our bodies after we have died, and to see clearly that we will dissolve back into the earth and disappear completely.

We might think that our personalities are here to stay, but if we look closer we find that although we have habit patterns that are deeply ingrained, they are also all subject to change. We all know people who have completely turned

176

their lives around, and dropped all kinds of behaviours that seemed an integral part of them. Some of us know what it feels like to fall in love or have a baby or be given a serious medical diagnosis – the things that were previously important can change almost overnight. Most of us explore familiar themes for long periods of our lives, learning to live with the abandonment we experienced as a small child, or trying to find a way of overcoming specific issues in our relationships, but even these 'groundhog day' experiences change very slightly every time we encounter them.

If there is no such thing as a permanent self and our 'self' is the vehicle we find ourselves travelling in, it's no wonder that we invest a considerable amount of energy into patching up the holes and making it 'solid'. We often use our stories about ourselves as our armour – maybe we buy into the illusion that we are self-sufficient and in control of what happens to us, or maybe we feel completely helpless and so refuse to take any action at all. We take refuge in our physical bodies and our personalities as if they will always be there.

Another characteristic of us human beings is that we don't deal very well with the unknown. It's usually more comfortable for us to jump to conclusions about what is happening rather than live with extended periods of uncertainty. We also like to have some certainty about 'who we are' – I am someone who can't draw, and who loves cats. When I'm presented with evidence that counters these theories, for example I am asked to do a sketch and it turns out well, or I'm really upset about my cats catching birds three nights in a row, I ignore this evidence as it doesn't fit neatly with the identity I have chosen for myself (or which I've grown into by default).

This mechanism works well in that it keeps us from feeling confused about who we are, and it gives us a measure of security. The downside is that it takes a lot of energy to keep repressing all the experiences which are counter to our personalities as we think we know them, and we also miss out on a big portion of life-as-it-actually-is, because there is no space for it in our conception of ourselves.

In this way the Dharma, the teachings of Buddhism, can be seen as helping us to loosen how compulsively locked on we are to our favourite substance – the illusion of a permanent self. If we can begin to loosen this addiction we will not only free up the energy we've been using to keep the truth at bay, but we'll also have access to more truth about ourselves and about the world. As the father of humanistic psychotherapy, Carl Rogers, said, 'The facts are always friendly, every bit of evidence one can acquire, in any area, leads one that much closer to what is true.'[28] It is better for us to know that we are sometimes good at drawing, as it opens us up to a creative hobby that we never thought would be possible. It's also better for us to know that we're not always kind, as we are more able to notice when we're mean to others and, as well as making the appropriate amends, be curious about why we feel the need to be mean and uncover some parts of ourselves that need attention.

Sitting with the truth of our impermanent selves is not comfortable. We have to develop a capacity for 'negative capability', that useful phrase first used by the poet Keats which describes '...when a man is capable of being in uncertainties, Mysteries, doubts, without any irritable

---

[28] Rogers, Carl R. *On Becoming a Person* (2004) Robinson

reaching after fact & reason...'[29] How do we get better at negative capability? By taking refuge in something that is more permanent than our selves – by taking refuge in the three jewels. Taking refuge allows us to feel that we are held, regardless of who we are or of what might happen. As our faith grows, our capacity for negative capability will increase. We will gradually get to know those parts of ourselves which have been hiding in the shadows, and we will become more intimate with the world too. Dharma is the truth of things-as-they-are. We are foolish beings and our bodies and our personalities are ever-changing. This doesn't mean that we can't enjoy being in our bodies right now, as they hold us upright and allows us to see the world and take in oxygen and food to keep them going. It doesn't mean we can't enjoy our quirks and preferences, without taking ourselves too seriously. Here we are. Let's make the most of it!

---

[29] Quoted in Bate, Walter Jackson *John Keats* (1964) Belknap Press

Pureland Buddhism and twelve-step programmes
Satyavani

Six years ago I walked into a room full of people who were there because they were deeply affected by someone else's drinking. I was terrified.

I was terrified because, by going in and sitting down in a circle with those people, I was admitting that I was one of them. I was so affected by someone else's drinking that I was going crazy. I wasn't in control of myself or the drinker. I admitted that I was powerless over alcohol, and that my life had become unmanageable. This is the first of the twelve steps which make up the twelve-step fellowships based on the Alcoholics Anonymous model.

Taking the second step, 'Came to believe that a power greater than ourselves could restore us to sanity', happened much more slowly. As I settled into the group and learnt how things worked, I realised that 'getting a sponsor' was a good thing to do. A sponsor would help you work through the twelve-steps on a one-to-one basis. You were meant to choose a person who had qualities that you wanted yourself – and I asked a confident woman called Suzanne if she'd sponsor me. She was tiny and blond and bubbly and to my horror when I went round to her house for my first meeting she talked a lot about God.

As you've already read, I'd always had an ambivalent relationship with religion. Suzanne said that she'd felt the same way when she first entered a twelve-step programme. The 'G' word had been a big trigger for her. Over time, she said she had started to see it as a signpost towards something ultimately unknowable. Using the word didn't mean that she had to swallow Christianity whole. She very slowly experimented with a relationship with something mysterious – something that possibly had more of the pieces of the puzzle than she did.

This is the concept of a Higher Power in the programme. As it says in step three, we are told that we do need a Higher Power, but we get to choose a Higher Power of our own conception – 'God as we understood God'. During step two we're not asked to take on a dogmatic belief in a particular kind of God. It's suggested that we 'come to believe' – that we enter a space where we are curious about our thoughts and feelings about a Higher Power, and where we leave some space for the possibility that if we can't do it on our own, there may be some help out there that will do a better job of running our lives.

The twelve-steps are an experiential programme – we are asked to try them out and to see what happens, rather like Buddha's suggestion that we make our own investigation of the truth rather than relying on the opinions of others (or our own mistaken opinions):

> Now, Kalamas, don't go by reports, by legends, by traditions, by scripture, by logical conjecture, by inference, by analogies, by agreement through pondering views, by probability, or by the thought, 'This contemplative is our teacher.' When you know

for yourselves that, 'These qualities are skillful; these qualities are blameless; these qualities are praised by the wise; these qualities, when adopted & carried out, lead to welfare & to happiness' — then you should enter and remain in them.[30]

This gentle encouragement to try things out allowed me, paradoxically, to hold onto enough of my power to feel safe enough to experiment with letting some of my power go.

Suzanne also said that it doesn't matter what our Higher Power is – the programme will work as long as we have one. She knew of a man who'd had his radiator as his Higher Power – when he was overwhelmed he'd hand his problems over to the radiator, and he'd listen to whatever the radiator might have to say when he was feeling stuck.

This step two work was the perfect preparation for my first visit to The Buddhist House in Narborough as a part of the psychotherapy training programme in 2007. I joined the morning services and when I encountered people doing prostrations and worshipping the Buddha I wasn't scared off as I would have been in my old atheist days. I was able to notice the qualities of the people practicing Pureland Buddhism – they seemed quietly confident, and happy. Just like in the twelve-step programme where we associate with the group members we want to emulate (one of AA's slogans is 'stick with the winners'), these Buddhists had something that I wanted and so I kept going to the services. I was reassured, as I was when I attended twelve-step meetings, that I didn't have to swallow any idea of a God-like Buddha straight away. Instead it was suggested that I live with the

---

[30] AN 3.65

new ideas and experiences for a while – to 'take what I like and leave the rest'.

This easy welcome allowed me to gradually find my way towards a faith in Amida Buddha that has changed my life. I've achieved things that I never could have dreamed of achieving if I hadn't taken the second step.

In his wonderful book *Recovery – The 12 Steps as Sacred Art*, Rami Shapiro says that of all the forms of Buddhism, Pureland is particularly suited to accompany those following a twelve-step programme.[31] With its emphasis on bombu nature and on other power, it encourages us to acknowledge our powerlessness through contrition, which puts us in a position where we can receive Amida's grace (which is always there). I am interested in the strong links between the twelve-step approach and a Pureland approach, both of which are counter-cultural in this age of 'do it yourself' and 'self-help'.

One way of summarising the whole twelve-steps is 'I can't, God can, let God'. The second step is the 'God can' part – becoming open to the concept that the Buddhas can help us where we can't help ourselves. Maybe we can also summarise Buddhism in this way, especially Pureland Buddhism. We come to some kind of limit, our 'rock bottom', and something in our ego is shattered. We lie in pieces on the floor, like Quan Yin after her failed attempt to heal all the suffering in the world, and then we call out for help. And then, gloriously, the Buddhas come. Our next challenge is to let them do what they will through us – their will, not ours, be done.

---

[31] Shaprio, Rami *Recovery – The 12 Steps as Sacred Art* (2009) SkyLight Paths

In my experience, there is a great relief in this way of approaching spirituality. We don't have to make it all happen! We can trust the Universe, and others, and the Buddhas. We don't have to take refuge in our own selves, and what's more, taking refuge in self is a really unhelpful thing to do.

Unfortunately, this knowledge doesn't seem to stick in my mind very well. I have to make the realisations over and over again – noticing when I'm 'playing God' (or making other people into God), handing that power back to where it belongs, and allowing myself to be shown the way by something bigger than me.

Adam practised with the Malvern Sangha and was an aspirant for a couple of years before 'switching track' and becoming a postulant, with the intention of taking the amitarya precepts.

I found Pureland Buddhism by accident whilst I was considering a possible means of deepening my already quite well established spiritual practice.

I had been working hard at incorporating twelve-step principles into my life for a few years as a solution to an addiction issue that I suffer with. The programme was working exactly as it had promised to work and I was free from my immediate, life impeding compulsions, facing life on life's terms. At two years into my recovery I started to experience some anxiety related symptoms which I couldn't ignore and sought some cognitive behavioural therapy in order to understand the cause of my distress. In doing so I was diagnosed with Post Traumatic Stress Disorder and advised to learn about the processes by which this illness manifests. This meant revisiting all of the childhood pain which I had managed, up until this point, to avoid with some success. I knew that the journey was going to be challenging and painful and with the help of my sponsor decided to start looking for a more intimate relationship with a power greater than myself to strengthen my recovery in the face of my new difficulties.

The obvious place to start seemed to be religion and so I increased my spiritual reading and viewing to include material from faith systems such as Buddhism and Christianity. I was already experiencing some internal resistance to the Christian faith which seemed to touch me in all the sensitive places and produce an attitude of rebellion which didn't seem in keeping with the desired effect. After a few weeks of research I felt a natural pull towards the story of Siddhartha the Indian sage who became a Buddha after renouncing a life of opulence in order to find the solution to the pain of existence. I was attracted to the pragmatic attitude and approach to what seems to be an impossible problem and was soon to find many layers of depth and complexity within the Buddhist philosophy which appealed to me even further.

As my sponsor and I scoured the shops for spiritual sustenance we bumped into a very happy and peaceful chap (Kaspa) in a local bookshop who told us about his Buddhist practice and that he was an ordained priest who practised in the local area. I had never heard of priesthood in Buddhism before, I had assumed that the religion was based on individual practice and required no spiritual authority or leadership other than that established by its founder 2500 years ago. We were invited to attend a service held by the priest and his wife in a town which we both knew.

For reasons beyond my control I couldn't get over to the service for some months but my sponsor started to attend regularly. Eventually the time came when I managed to find my way there and all of my expectations were surpassed. My confidence in religion as an organised spirituality had been shaken to some extent and although my sponsor had expressed his interest to me based on his visits, I had imagined a tedious and half-hearted gathering where people could breeze in and out and no commitment or responsibility was required. What I found was the polar opposite: a well organised and established gathering of devoted practitioners, all of whom seemed to be settled and confident in their faith. The ceremonies were somewhat different to anything that I'd ever experienced and a certain amount of open mindedness was required in order to appreciate the meaning behind them. I was impressed by the level and quality of awareness which these people displayed, an air of conscientiousness was operating at the heart of all the practice and social interactions which I found very stimulating and refreshing.

The only real first-hand experience of Buddhist practice I had had was a weekend retreat in a meditation centre years ago which I had attended under the influence of some powerful drugs – needless to say, the essence of the practice had passed me by. Since then and with a sober mind I had read about the Buddhist philosophy which encourages discipline of the mind as conducive to and coextensive with universal peace and had engaged deeply in efforts to quiet my own busy head with practices such as mindfulness which produced some very encouraging results. It was interesting to find that these Buddhists called themselves 'Pureland' Buddhists and looked to a higher Buddha for salvation via a simple mantra which was recited pretty much continuously throughout the services. The simplicity of the practice combined with the pleasant atmosphere was enough to hold my interest and I soon found myself making the 50 minute journey to the service once a week every week, or as often as I could.

When something takes my interest, as Pureland Buddhism did and still does, I have no difficulty engaging with it on every level available to me. I quite quickly immersed myself in the practices and started to have very lovely experiences. I got involved in whatever way was possible for me and it is presently the biggest part of my life. I currently travel from Sangha to Sangha and am training to be an Amitarya in the Amida Order.

Pureland Buddhism turned out to be exactly the path that I had been searching for. Revering a specific deity by means of practices which don't require years of arduous training allowed me to quickly attain the sense of union and intimacy that I had sought from the religious path. I developed a relationship with the Buddha which allows me to bring him into all of my affairs, keeping me grounded in the good stuff as well as the struggles. I've learned that my pain is not always a problem to be transcended but often the way in which I relate to the Buddha and all the holy beings of the universe, and my inherent and persistent foolishness provides the terms on which I seek Buddha, the God of my understanding. Namo Amida Bu.

Ethics as a container for awakening
Kaspalita

Buddhism is full of precepts. There are the traditional rules for monks and nuns, the five lay precepts, and many other lists of ideals from the six perfections to the eightfold path. As part of my own ordination ceremony I agreed that it was my intention to keep over a hundred and fifty precepts.

How do we relate to all of these ideas? At first glance sometimes they can appear like a list of rules and regulations to keep ourselves in line.

Thinking of rules and regulations reminds me of the attitude to precepts in the Christian tradition I was part of as a child. I appreciate that there are many traditions of Christianity and many different churches, and not all of them treat the precepts in this way – but there was something of the 'be good or you're going to hell' in the way I was taught.

I remember a line of a song from Sunday School, 'Envy, jealousy malice, pride: they must never in your heart abide.' I don't think it was explicitly spelled out what would happen if you did have these qualities in your heart, but it was *something bad.* So whenever I was envious or jealous or malicious or proud I pretended that I wasn't and locked them away deep in my unconscious mind.

Even so there was something inspiring about having an ideal way of behaving to aspire to, and sometimes that kept me on the straight and narrow. However it also supported the part of me that judged others, and I ended up looking down on people who weren't behaving as I thought they should be, which made it much more difficult for me to relate to others.

There was some of this attitude around in medieval Japan too, with landlords using threats of hell, or a lower rebirth, to keep their serfs in line.

How else might we approach the precepts?

There are several different ways of thinking about the precepts which I like.

Precepts are training

In the most literal translation of the five lay precepts, they begin with the words, 'I undertake the training to....'

I like this attitude of training. It suggests an acceptance of our current state, as well as an acknowledgment that there is need for improvement. The idea of training is very different to the idea of 'follow these or else'. When you are a trainee you begin knowing by very little and having little skill, and as you progress your knowledge and skills increase. We are always training in the precepts – moving towards the direction of understanding and following them, but never completely inhabiting them until we become Buddhas ourselves, in some future lifetime.

Even in Hell there is a Buddha

The Buddhist Wheel of Life illustrates all of the different realms one can be reborn into, from the realms of the gods to the human and animal realms to the various hells. If you look at a Wheel of Life closely you will see that in every realm there is a Buddha, even in the hell realms where you can find demons boiling people in cauldrons of hot oil (I wouldn't want to be the demon or the person). Liberation is possible even from the worst of places, and even in the worst of places there will be a Buddha loving you.

This undermines the old idea I had of religious vows. Although there will be consequences to our actions, which may include a trip to hell, salvation is always nearby.

The Precepts are the Buddha

One way that Dharmavidya encourages us to understand the precepts is by seeing that they describe what a Buddha is and how a Buddha behaves in the world. The precepts are an indication of what a Buddha would do in this world.

With this understanding we can use studying the precepts to deepen our experience of nembutsu. Studying the precepts brings us closer to the Buddha, and studying the actions we take in the world, often in contrast to the precepts, brings us closer to an understanding of our bombu nature.

In this way the precepts become a container for our own awakening.

The Precepts and Faith

Another way that Dharmavidya has spoken about working with the precepts is related to faith. Every time we fail to keep a precept it is a failure of faith. When our faith in the Buddha is complete we follow the precepts naturally: we respond to whatever is in front of us with a loving heart.

What stops our heart being full of faith is the fear that leads to greed, hate and delusion; fear of the unknown, fear of being out of control, fear of dukkha, or fear that the Buddha isn't there. When we act from fear we act selfishly, and the precepts are broken.

We do sometimes feel the fear of those existential issues keenly. However, it's more common for our strongest fears to appear in specific moments. We are more afraid (and therefore more greedy, hateful and so on) in some situations and of some things than in others.

If we think of the precepts in this way, whenever we notice that we are falling short, we can take it as an opportunity to investigate the specific failure of faith. What was the fear? When did it arise? And so on. We can also use this as an opportunity to bring ourselves closer to the Buddha, not only the act of simply remembering the Buddha, but allowing the Buddha to be kind and loving to whatever part of us is afraid. In this way our faith increases, and we may be able to keep the precepts more closely in the future.

Contrition

In the *Summary of Faith and Practice,* which we recite during our morning service, we read that, 'Saving grace, as was made clear by Shan Tao's dream and advice to Tao Cho, only comes through the sange-mon.'

Sange-mon means the gate of contrition and it is considered an essential element of Pureland practice. Contrition is not guilt that we carry around with us like a stick we use to beat ourselves up over and over again, but rather a genuine recognition of our faults and the harm we have caused. This real seeing of our human nature, both in

194

the general case and in specific moments, may be accompanied by all sorts of feelings including guilt, anger and blame, but genuine contrition moves towards sadness, fellow-feeling and a recognition that we are loved even though we are a being that causes harm.

When we cause some harm in the world, to another person or to our environment, these actions and the way we treat them can get between us and the Buddha.

Tao Cho, who lived in the 6th and 7th Centuries, was a Chinese Buddhist Master, a scholar of Pureland Buddhism, a builder of many temples, and the teacher of Shan Tao. Towards the end of his life, he started to have the feeling that he was not going to be born into the Pureland. He felt weighed down with something, although he couldn't put his finger on what it was. There was something coming between him and the Buddha; something taking up the space where his faith had been.

One day he told his disciple Shan Tao about these feelings. That night Shan Tao had a dream about his teacher. In the dream he understood that about all the insects and small creatures he may have harmed or killed during his prolific temple building. In the morning he spoke to Tao Cho and suggested a public confession. Tao Cho realised that what his student was saying was true, and made an act of contrition in public. Supported by that ritual he was able to see his own nature clearly and to feel accepted by Amida Buddha just as he was. He felt once more that his rebirth in the Pureland was assured.

It is the various forms of selfishness that fill up the space where faith also wants to live, and squeezes it out; from the greed and anger that motivate selfish acts in the first place, to the resistance we have to accepting our selfish nature.

This resistance to seeing our foolish nature can cause more problems than the initial selfish impulse. If we act rashly in a moment of anger or greed, and see ourselves clearly, we have the chance to bring that part of ourselves in relationship to the Buddha – to feel that part of us is accepted – and it is in that moment that we might be able to let go of that selfishness. Paradoxically the more acceptable or loveable we feel, just as we are, the less likely we are to engage in acts which would make it harder for ordinary people to accept us.

It can be difficult for us to accept that we have greedy and hateful parts of ourselves, or difficult to accept the consequences they lead to. Perhaps we are afraid of the feelings that will come up when we truly look at our own nature. Or perhaps we feel that if we really own those selfish impulses we will be rejected by those people we love, or the groups that we want to be a part of. In Pureland Buddhism we are able to be contrite, to take an honest look at ourselves and feel a tenderness towards our selfishness, because we trust that the Buddha is there feeling tender towards us.

Sometimes the Sangha can model this for us. The people that we practice with are able to accept and love us, even the parts of ourselves that we find difficult to love. Occasionally we act so wildly that the Sangha might struggle to love us, or might take a while to get in touch with the love they have for us. This is why taking refuge in the Buddhas is at the heart of our practice. Even the best human beings are not perfectly loving all of the time, but the Buddhas can do this.

In our darkest moments we can always turn towards the Buddha and know that they love us just as we are.

This is not just an abstract statement.

Back in my first or second year of practicing Pureland Buddhism, when I was staying at Dharmavidya's old farmhouse in France one summer I had a powerful experience of feeling held by the Buddha. I don't remember what, if anything, sparked it off. It wasn't in the shrine room, in fact I think I may have been alone, in one of the small animal houses that have been converted into monastic, cell-like bedrooms. Perhaps I was thinking about some selfish acts I had performed in the past, perhaps these feelings came out of the blue, perhaps I had been primed by beginning to feel accepted by the community I was living in. Whatever, I suddenly had a felt sense of the presence of the Buddha: something in the universe that could love me just as I was. I remember feeling profoundly undeserving and loved anyway. I saw myself in all my selfishness being loved by the Buddha, and it was unbelievable. It was a powerful and moving experience.

Not all experiences of contrition and of feeling close to the Buddha are as dramatic as that one.

My experience of the Buddha these days is often of a much quieter presence, and a sense of trusting that something is there to love me.

Hopefully I have given you a sense that the precepts, and other ideals in Buddhism, are a useful tool which can help move you towards liberation, rather than a set of rules that you will be judged against and condemned or commended.

The precepts are a jewelled boat to cross the river of desire. They are a divine carriage to traverse the mountain of hatred. They are an immediate cause of entering the citadel of awakening. They are a direct path leading to the realm of the Buddhas. It is because of the precepts that the sustaining power of the Three Jewels, leading all beings to enlightenment, is forever fresh and new. The means of training thus provided for all kinds of beings has great saving virtue.[32]

[32] Gyonen *The Essentials of the Vinaya Tradition and The Collected Teachings of the Tendai Lotus School* Tr. Pruden, Leo and Swanson, Paul (1995) BDK America

The Dharma of tea towels

Satyavani

It was never in my plan to live in a building with people other than my husband. And yet here I am sharing a big house with five other men – some of whom I knew pretty well when they moved in, and some of whom I didn't.

We're not a full-time training community like the Buddhist community Kaspa lived in for several years – we only eat together once a week, and Kaspa and I have a self-contained flat where we can disappear and cook for ourselves. However whenever there are shared spaces, there are opportunities for us to bump up against each other....

In the communal kitchen there is a basket where everyone puts tea towels when they are dirty. We have a lot of tea towels. As we spent our first weeks in the temple they seemed to be piling up fast. I washed them, hung them all out, folded them and put them back in the drawer. Then I did another load. Then I watched the basket pile up again. Would anyone else do them?

I passed the dirty tea towels every day, and resentment started building. I mentioned the huge teetering pile in a house meeting for a second time. The next day I went to the laundry room to do some of our own washing. Someone had washed the tea towels, and then forgot all about them and disappeared for the weekend. They sat in the drum smelling strongly of damp. If I wanted to do my own washing, I'd have to wash them again and hang them all out....

As I hung them out I laughed. It was as if the Buddhas had arranged a little lesson for me. You can't get out of washing these tea towels, you know. And look – now you're doing it, and it's not so bad is it?

I realised that it wasn't really the tea towels I was resentful about at all. Behind the resentment was fear. One of the things I felt anxious about before we moved in was how I would manage to share space with others without ending up feeling responsible for *everything* that needed doing. Others won't notice things-that-need-doing in the way I do. I will have to slave away and everyone else will be sitting around drinking tea and I will become completely overwhelmed.

Of course, I carry this story around with me wherever I go. The reality is that the people I share this space with do help out in all kinds of ways. We occasionally need to remind people to do certain things and this has felt fine. Everything here runs extraordinarily smoothly.

The tea towels showed me where my fear was, and then (with the help of my housemate) they showed me how I could let go and have faith. Whether or not I end up washing all the tea towels, everything will be okay.

This is what happens in Sangha. The value of Sangha, our spiritual community, is that we are all on a spiritual path together. We are able to support each other in our spiritual training – sometimes consciously, by encouraging each other, or sometimes holding each other to account, and sometimes by rubbing people up the wrong way. Some of the most useful (and occasionally painful) lessons I've learnt about myself and how I operate in the world have been through seeing myself reflected back by other people.

Whenever I have a strong emotion in response to someone else there is an opportunity to learn – why does this matter so much to me? What am I avoiding, or what do I need to protect myself from? What is going on when I feel disappointed or confused or irritated or sad or furious or over-excited....

Yesterday I passed the tea towel basket. It wasn't quite full, but I was on my way to my office so I put them in the washing machine on my way past. As I hung them out afterwards, I enjoyed the neat rectangles and their fresh smell. As I folded them back into the drawer I enjoyed the satisfaction of knowing that my temple-mates would have clean tea towels to dry their plates.

Wherever there is grit, there is the potential for a new opalescent layer of pearl.

What or who is bothering you at the moment? What fear is it pointing towards? How might you let go into faith?

Richard is a retired teacher who is currently working towards a doctorate on the teachings of Dharmavidya and Honen. He teaches on our Vow 22 programme and is a Lay Order member.

After increasing dissatisfaction with aspects of another school which I had been practising in for many years I stumbled across Modgala on an Amida stall at Leamington Peace Festival. After this, I attended a few events at the Buddhist House at Narborough, met Kaspa, Susthama and a few others and was immediately impressed by the warmth and the structured informality of the approach. I was also looking for a bit of 'academic' training in Buddhism and I found Vow 22! I was pleased that the laity (not just the ordained religious) are held, valued and nurtured in Amidism. Also (and very importantly for my own personal practice) room is made for the Divine Feminine (in the form of Kuan Yin) in our practice – a rare thing in our predominantly 'man made' religious world.

What do I like about Amida-shu? Just about everything really! The simplicity and accessibility of the central practice (the nembutsu) is a truly wondrous thing and unfolds in each individual practitioner in their own way, and in accord with their own needs and personality: it gives people ownership of their own religious practice without the central control of doctrine 'from above'.

For my practice I read Chapter 25 of the Lotus Sutra (obsessive again, but I love this writing so much!) every morning plus the Invocation from the Amida morning service. I also chant silently in my head for about 15 minutes when I get up. At our monthly Amida Birmingham meetings we do Morning Service and chanting. I also go to retreats when I can.

How does it help me? Quite simply, it puts my own concerns into a wider perspective. It helps me get out of bed in the morning. I hope it makes me more loving. It gives me a chant with which to distract my otherwise obsessively anxious mind and rest itself on.

Spiritual materialism
Kaspalita

> The pursuit of self-advantage and gain has a clear and pervasive logic. It can enter into every crevice of one's life, not excluding one's spiritual path. This is what Chögyam Trungpa Rinpoche described with the potent phrase 'spiritual materialism'.[33]

What is spiritual materialism? Spiritual materialism is realising that your ego has taken a spark of compassion and diverted it from its goal, and instead used that energy to maintain some defensive thought pattern or another.

Sometimes that energy is completely diverted and the original impulse is lost completely, and sometimes pride or fear and compassion appear together.

A few days ago I was leading the morning service here. Before going into the shrine room I caught sight of myself in one of the large ornately framed mirrors that we inherited when we bought the temple building. I don't get to see what I look like in robes very often. I look like a priest, I thought, formal and with an air of spiritual authority. In that moment I decided that I wanted to do a really good job of leading the service.

---

[33] Brazier, David *The Inner Logic of Other Power* Tricycle (Spring 2015)

I paid attention to every footstep and gesture as I made offerings at the shrine, I pitched the chant at just the right note and considered deeply what speed of walking meditation would be best for this particular group of people. And then as we were reciting the morning liturgy I missed out a line and the whole chant broke down. I have been doing this long enough to recognise that this sort of thing happens sometimes, and was able to take my mistake in good humour. My inflated ego was bought back down to earth with a bump.

Spiritual materialism is the ego subverting spiritual practice (or in this case, spiritual authority) for its own ends. When this happens, we will get shown up at some point. The ego resists reality and spiritual practice brings us closer to what is real. In spiritual materialism, the practice becomes a tool of the ego and takes us away from what is real, but reality cannot be avoided forever.

When reality bursts the ego bubble it is usually not a pleasant experience, but it is a great opportunity to see ourselves and our bombu nature clearly.

Spiritual friendship

Satyavani

Shakyamuni Buddha's faithful assistant, Ananda, once said to him, 'Lord, I think that half of the Holy Life is spiritual friendship, association with the Lovely.' The Buddha replied: 'That's not so; say not so, Ananda. It is not half of the Holy Life, it is the whole of the Holy Life.'[34]

It is difficult for us to practise alone, or to live a spiritual life without any support. We are strongly affected by our conditions, and if all our friends eat meat or spend their leisure time in the pub it's hard to be the odd one out. This is why it's important to see if we can find at least one or two friends who will support us on our path – who will encourage us to keep going and maybe gently challenge us when we lose our way.

Spiritual friendship and Sangha is also important because it's in relationship that we learn the most about ourselves. Ajahn Chah, a leading teacher in the Thai Forest Tradition, found that he could develop profound states of mind when he was meditating in the hills on his own, but that when he came back to live with the other monks he couldn't go for long without losing his patience with them and getting annoyed. After a few years he realised he had something to learn, and stayed in community more and

---

[34] SN 45.2

more. He went on to develop his monasteries in this style. I have had the same experience after coming out of retreat feeling calm and slightly smug, and then spending a day with my family!

Looking for friends who support you on your own path doesn't mean finding people who are practising the same religion as you, or even people with any spiritual dimensions to their lives. When you spend time in the company of particular friends, you will find yourself becoming a better version of yourself (or at least feeling inspired to be). These are the people who understand what it means to be human and who accept you as you are, but who also have faith in you and who cheer you on. Colluding with others and having them collude with us is a comforting pastime, but the effects are short-lived and this kind of ignorance leads us away from the truth of reality. Spiritual friends help us to face the sometimes harsh reality of life and of our own foolish nature head on, without losing heart. It is through facing these realities that we become open to grace.

For all these reasons there is a strong culture in the Amida Sangha of coming together and sharing practice and our struggles, joy and vulnerabilities. This culture of friendship is difficult to convey in a book – you might get more of a taste of it if you came to one of our services, or sat in a listening circle with an atmosphere of tenderness.... Maybe one day you'll come and stay in our temple or attend a practice group and you can experience it for yourself.

Until then, I'll try and give you a taste for it by describing a day from a retreat that took place in Dharmavidya's hermitage in France. The hermitage is an old farm house in a large plot of land including woods, fields and a bamboo patch. The shrine room is in a barn with a big open entrance so you feel as if you are half inside the building and half connected to the garden and the open skies. Being on retreat allows Amida-shu members from around the world to live as a community for weeks at a time. It is both a place from which we draw sustenance and a safe space which allows 'stuff' to come up! Join us as the day begins....

A Day on Retreat in Bessait-Le-Fromental, June 2015

7.15 a.m. The day begins with the ringing of the waking bell, carried by Maitrisimha (a long-standing member of our Dutch Sangha) all the way around the site. Adam is kneading bread in the kitchen, others are still sleeping. I am bell-master today and so I'm already in the shrine room where I'm sweeping the bits of grass and twigs from the old carpets on the hard dirt floor, cleaning the shrines and making sure there's enough incense and candles for morning service. Jnanamati is in another corner of the shrine room, chanting the *Larger Pure Land Sutra*, one of the key texts in our tradition. His voice drones like a buzzing insect, occasionally lifting to accent various words. I feel moved that he is doing this practice for all of us.

At 7.45 a.m. I ring the big golden gong outside the barn to call people to service. We assemble in the shrine room, some of us sitting on a hotchpotch of old cushions, some on chairs. The main shrine is a very large piece of flat stone from the land somewhere. I wonder who put it there and how it was carried. There is a small golden Buddha, his paint worn off in places, resting on an intensely blue piece of satin which is new this year. There are also smaller shrines around the hall – one for Quan Shi Yin, an ancestor shrine, one for Samantabhadra (who rides an elephant) and one for Maitreya, Buddha of the Future. Each shrine has a tea-light and a place where incense can be offered.

The steady rhythm of the *mokugyo* begins (a traditional Japanese wooden instrument in the shape of a fish, struck with a mallet to produce a hollow 'donk') and we chant 'Namo Amida Bu' until the celebrant enters the shrine room and we all stand and bow. Morning service consists of the celebrant making offerings, walking meditation whilst chanting, silent sitting, prostrations, liturgy and a Dharma talk. Afterwards we file out into the sunshine which is already hot. Ordained members fold their robes (a large square of red or red and yellow material stitched together) by resting the middle edge on their head whilst grasping hold of the two corners. We move from the formal atmosphere of the shrine room to greeting each other, asking our friends if they slept well or if they had to remove any ticks from their legs or stomachs. We are close to nature here and the facilities are basic. This requires a certain hardiness from retreatants, and it is also a reminder of how many home comforts we usually take for granted.

9 a.m. The gong rings again to summon us for breakfast. The food is blessed before we line up and help ourselves to what we want. Nala the dog waits patiently for the blessing to finish, thinking she might find a tasty morsel somewhere with all this delicious food around. Floor has made vegan chocolate pancakes and I feel spoilt as I take a bowl of oats and fruit soaked in fruit juice (with walnuts fresh from the tree) and pancakes and a cup of tea to the picnic tables where we eat whenever the weather allows. After breakfast the crockery and kitchenware is all carried to a table outside where the washing up is done (there isn't any

space inside) and four of us stand around washing, rinsing, drying and taking full trays back into the kitchen. All the best and juiciest conversations happen around the washing up table!

10 a.m. The gong rings for our first session of the day. Adam and Floor return to the kitchen to get started on lunch, and the rest of us convene on plastic chairs in the shade under the big walnut tree. The attic space we usually use for meeting, full of comfy old sofas in a patchwork of colours, is already too hot. The shade is delicious and the breeze is cool. The downside is the occasional deer fly who won't take no for an answer and return again and again to prick our skin. Today we are sharing reports from various Amida Sanghas around the world including Canada, London, Belgium, Hawaii, and our temple in Malvern. It is good to hear how they are all thriving in their own way, and particularly moving to hear of a pilgrimage to Shakyamuni's birthplace made by our ordained priests in India including Suando in her colourful robes amongst ten coach-loads of Theravadan monks, all in orange and all men.

Earlier in the week we had discussions around faith – our own personal histories of faith, what having faith feels like, how it moves us to act in our daily lives. We also talk about the 'state of the Order' – what stage are we in in our development as a Sangha, how things are changing, what might need attention. A lot of the change is seen as a natural unfolding – we can put ourselves in good conditions, but we can't control the speed or even the direction of what the Sangha is developing into. We try to take this approach here at Malvern – what is the building asking us to do next? Is the community ready to take on more responsibility? We try to be led by an 'other-power' rather than thinking we know best and trying to force or control things.

As our meetings progress we all get to know each other better – hearing each other's struggles, recognising difficulties from our own lives and understanding more about why we each find different things difficult. There is also space in the meetings for difficult emotions – I find myself exploding one afternoon in an angry and hurt outburst, trusting the group to hold the strength of my emotion. There are sometimes disagreements or struggles between different pairs of group members as buttons are pushed, and sadness and loss can well up when we least expect it to. As human beings we often just have to push forwards in the dark, not knowing why we feel so strongly or exactly how we're getting tangled up with each other. Mostly we come through to a deeper understanding of ourselves or each other, and can see each other with compassion, but not always. We are not immune to the difficulties faced by all human beings in relationships and in groups. Being in relationship is scary, and sometimes I feel that the closer I get to this bunch of disparate people, the more terrified I become. Luckily Amida is there as a bigger container, so when Sangha members do let me down (just as I will let others down) I can rest in a bigger faith. All will be well.

11.30 a.m. During our break Kaspa takes the toilet paper to be burnt. A strained sewage system means we are putting our used toilet paper in bags rather than down the toilet. I feel grateful that others are taking this job on, and wonder why I have been so squeamish about doing it myself. We are usually protected from these facts of life.

2 p.m. Our second session after lunch is a stone passing, giving us all a chance to share whatever is in our

hearts before three of our group leave first thing the next morning. It's a simple mechanism – handing someone a stone so everyone listens to them without interrupting. The quality of attention that results always seems to lead to a sacred and intimate 'coming together'.

It is 39 degrees. When the stone passing is finished there is time for a quick visit to a local lake, packed with children and their families as it's after school. We wade in and push out into the water which is surprisingly warm on top but with cooler currents underneath. On other days we will help around the site – doing some strimming, weeding or watering. Being in a Sangha means making time to have fun as well as practising, working and sharing together.

6.30 p.m. The gong goes again for dinner – a delicious lentil shepherd's pie – followed by a fruit ice lolly which is very welcome as the stubborn heat hangs around into the evening. The food has been particularly good during this retreat and has included a few trays of brownies. I think I may return heavier than when I arrived. Eating together is an important part of being in community – sharing food from the same pot, and sitting down to eat it without a television. At our temple here in Malvern we eat together with the house-mates every Friday night, and this has proved to be an important way of keeping in touch with each other, especially in such a big house where some of us go for days without seeing each other.

8 p.m. The last time I will ring the gong today, to summon people to evening service. We walk around the shrine room chanting 'Amitabha' and I am struck afresh by the simplicity of this practice – all we need to do is say the name of Amida Buddha. The candles glow as the light seeps out of the evening, and a couple of sparrows fly above our

heads from rafter to rafter, going about their business. We finish by chanting the evening liturgy:

> By the grace that I receive
> Through Amitabha's vows
> May I be moved to deeds
> For the benefit of all....

How many times have I sung these lines in this space, surrounded by these people, or others from around the world? Like a child's favourite story book read over and over, the power of ritual increases every time we perform it. A deep sense of gratitude sinks into me and, not uncommonly during practice here, I am moved to tears.

9.30 p.m. A final cup of chicory (or chic-choc, a mixture of chicory and drinking chocolate popularised by Dharmavidya!) on chairs out the front of the house. Talk is of Sangha members not present, the weather, ferry strikes, Greek Gods, our cats at home without us. We are finally driven inside by mosquitos and tiredness, Kaspa and I up to our attic bedroom, cooler because of the shiny silver insulation taped up onto the sloping ceiling. There was a scurrying inside the wall last night which woke me up and made me nervous – maybe a bat – but tonight all is quiet. I read for a short while and then we turn off the light. We sleep deeply.

Prajnatara is a minister in London, Canada and runs an established Sangha with her husband James (a Lay Order member). She works as a therapist and worked in a University for many years.

I found Pureland Buddhism as the result of taking the Long Distance Buddhist Psychology program. After graduating I lost contact with the Amida community and then one day I went online to see if 'they' still existed. Lo and behold, there they were, and now connected with Pureland Buddhism. I knew little about the Pureland tradition and was intrigued. The rest is history.

Pureland Buddhism is messy, lively, relational, heart-centred, and joyful. I feel I can relax here. I am far more accepting of my faults and the faults of others – less inclined to demand perfection. I sense the Buddhas around me, and recognize them in the faces of others, nature, the written word, my dreams, and so on. I live in the company of the Buddhas and Bodhisattvas.

Liturgy and recitation of the nembutsu are my go to practices. I also have a visualization whereby I end each day by putting all my cares and feelings of gratitude in the lap of the Buddha. I also fill my external world with images of the Buddha.

There is a deep peace that accompanies those who entrust themselves to Amida. Despite our flaws, and our inability to live up to the best of our intentions, we are called

by Love. Amida hooks us and we live thereafter by grace.
How blessed we are.

Practice

The central practice of Amida-shu is nembutsu, the chanting of the Name of Amida Buddha, usually in the form Namo Amida Bu, using tones, rhythms, melodies and choreographies. The practice expresses religious feeling. There is nothing calculating or spiritually ambitious about it. Whether we enter the Pure Land is a matter of grace, not achievement. The Tathagata pours down the rain of Dharma on great and poor, good and bad, alike. How we are affected depends upon our karmic condition, but grace cuts through karma. The nembutsu is a call from the human condition toward the sacred, from this to That.

Dharmavidya

Nembutsu
Kaspalita

Nembutsu is the practice of calling the name of Amida Buddha, or of saying the name of the Buddha in recognition that you have already heard his call. Nembutsu is an English transliteration of a Japanese word that is a translation of the Chinese word *Nienfo*. It is the practice we use to connect with something completely wise and loving that is outside the experience of our own small mind.

We believe that there have been many Buddhas, not just the historical Shakyamuni who lived and died in India and Nepal two and half thousand years ago. The Buddha we choose to bring to mind when practising nembutsu is Amida Buddha, the Buddha of limitless light and life.

Shakyamuni Buddha told a story about Amida Buddha, saying that all beings that heard the name of Amida Buddha, with faith in their heart, would be reborn in Amida's Pure Land of love and bliss and from there become a fully enlightened being.

We can take this on its own terms – or think of it as a powerful myth that tells us something true and important about the nature of the universe and salvation.

In early Chinese Buddhism, the primary way of connecting to Amida Buddha was through visualisation practices. Nembutsu was bringing the Buddha to mind by creating an image of the Buddha in your mind's eye and then meditating upon that image. As well as visualisation practices there was also nembutsu recitation practice. In China this meant chanting 'Namo Omito Fo'. Although visualisation had been seen as the most powerful way to invoke Amida, in the 7th Century Shan Tao (or Shandao), a Chinese Buddhist Master, realised that saying the name of Amida was enough to make a connection with that Buddha and guarantee rebirth in his Pure Land.

In medieval Japan there were various practices associated with Amida Buddha including recitation, but the idea of reciting the name as being sufficient for rebirth in the Pure Land had been lost until Honen rediscovered this idea through Shan Tao's writing. Honen went on to teach recitation of Amida's name as the unique and essential practice for rebirth in the Pure Land. Other practices were helpful and good for their own sake, he taught, but as foolish beings of wayward passion the only way to guarantee our enlightenment is to rely on the power of Amida Buddha, and we can do this through reciting his name.

Shan Tao and Honen's idea of practicing verbal nembutsu may have come from reading the sutras and commentaries, but it was confirmed through their experience of the practice. I'm sure they both had a sense of being close to Amida and that they understood the nembutsu practice had created the conditions for this closeness. Honen had visions of Amida and the Pure Land throughout his life.

My own experience of the practice is that it creates a container for our relationship to the Buddha, or that it keeps turning us back to Amida's light. We do not always see the light consciously, or feel close to the Buddha; sometimes our practice is clouded by frenetic thoughts, by greed, hate and delusion, but even in the midst of this we are being bathed in the light.

Whilst Honen emphasised practice, reciting the name daily and making special time for continuous nembutsu practice, Shinran, a disciple of Honen, emphasised faith, or the attitude of the practitioner. For Shinran the essential attitude was understanding that rebirth in the Pure Land, and thus enlightenment, was assured because Amida Buddha, a fully enlightened realized being of great power, was working on our behalf.

Honen rejected the 'Buddha-nature' argument, that all beings had the potential to become a Buddha themselves, as in Japan at that time it was suggested that ordinary people couldn't realise their Buddha-nature, only ordained monks. Shinran re-imagined Buddha-nature as Amida's power working for each of us. We all have Buddha-nature, Shinran taught, in the sense that Amida is holding each of us in mind and will take us into his Pure Land. All we have to do is recognise that this is true and rebirth is assured. In this way of thinking, nembutsu becomes a rejoicing and a way of saying thank you for our guaranteed salvation, rather than a means to that salvation.

In Amida-shu we practise nembutsu with both of these attitudes; as a way of connecting with or tuning into Amida Buddha, and as a way of being grateful for our assured liberation by the Buddha's power.

To ask if Amida Buddha is a real being sitting and practising in a land where the trees are made from precious gems (as his Pure Land is described) is to miss the most important point.

The promise of Amida Buddha that has been handed down to us points to what Dharmavidya has called a 'benign process' at work in the universe. Not only are we acceptable to this benign process just as we are, but if we come into closer relationship with it, if we become participants in this process, our own liberation from dukkha is assured, and we become part of something bigger. The more we participate in this benign process, the more we will become a part of the causes and conditions for others to be caught up in this process.

This is what the nembutsu points to and aligns us to: the power of enlightenment working its way through the universe, liberating countless beings. As we invite this energy into our lives we become part of the dance of enlightenment.

If you come and practise with us, you will hear the nembutsu chanted in many different forms in our services. The most usual form is 'Namo Amida Bu'. As well as hearing this chanted in services, you will also hear it spoken when people meet each other in the corridor, or when something goes wrong, or when something goes well.

Each time we recite the name of Amida we are reminding ourselves of the Buddha's promise to save all beings, and of the benign process of enlightenment at work in the world.

At home people recite nembutsu with a mala, or chant along to recordings of other's chanting, or simply say 'Namo Amida Bu' as they remember the Buddha throughout the day.

If you have your own mala you could make a daily practice of sitting and reciting 108 nembutsu each day, simply by saying 'Namo Amida Bu', or using one of the melodies we use when chanting nembutsu. Or you could download some of those chants and sing along with them for ten or twenty minutes a day.

Honen used to chant continually throughout the day, keeping it going in his own mind when he was chatting to people or just going about his business. He said that he would chant 60 000 nembutsu each day in this way. This kind of intense practice might be completely outside of your experience – but sometimes you might want to experiment with filling your mind with the Buddha throughout the whole day in this way.

Honen also encouraged his followers to make special times to put everything aside and just practise nembutsu for an extended period of time. We do this with our continuous chanting days that Satya has written about elsewhere. I find it an invaluable way of deepening my own practice, and my experiences during those practice days remind me of the power of nembutsu.

Despite this practice, Honen also said that one nembutsu is enough, as it is Amida's power that liberates us. The extended periods of practice just help us to remember this.

Nembutsu is a way of keeping the Buddha in mind, and remembering that the saving grace of Amida is close to hand. Whatever brings us back to this knowledge can be a form of nembutsu, from a continuous recitation practice to simply having an image of the Buddha above our desk at work.

Having a shrine
Satyavani

As human beings we often forget what is fundamentally important (loving each other, doing what good we can with the time we have) and get caught up in the minutiae of our lives. Have I replied to that urgent email? What did he think about me when I said that? What will I cook for dinner?

Human beings are also powerfully conditioned by objects, and so one of the best ways of staying in relationship with something more meaningful than these mundane concerns is to surround ourselves with good objects. We do this when we have pictures of our loved ones on our desk at work, art on our walls that inspires us, or houseplants that connect us to nature.

The objects that work as an ultimate reminder for Buddhists are representations of the Buddha. These statues, whether they are huge and golden and sent as a gift from Thailand, like the Buddha on our main shrine, or made of plastic and £5.99 from a home furnishings store, point me towards something in the universe that is infinitely wise and compassionate. This is what I want to be in relationship with, and conditioned by. This is where I have the best chance of the Buddha's qualities rubbing off on me as I experience myself in his field of merit.

A shrine is a further elaboration on bringing these good qualities into our homes. As we tend to them and spend time in front of them over time, spiritual associations build up and the shrine becomes more and more sacred. All rituals are designed to help us to deepen our connection with something – each other or particular phenomena – and the rituals we carry out around Buddhist artefacts help to strengthen our connection with the Buddhas. Shrines can be places where we spend 'quality time' with the Buddha, maybe sitting quietly in meditation, or asking for advice, or handing our problems over to the Buddha so he can help us to carry them.

How can you make yourself a Buddhist shrine? First get yourself a central statue or object – a Buddha rupa that you feel a connection with. Find a good place for your shrine – the top of a bookcase, a shelf or a table. I like to make shrines where they take a central position – not off in the corner of the room. It's also good to have space in front of the shrine where you can sit or make prostrations.

You might want to find a cloth to place underneath the Buddha, to represent the ground, and if you like you could have a figure on either side of the Buddha to represent his attendants Quan Shi Yin and Tai Shih Chih (or the Pureland ancestors Shan Tao and Honen).

When you approach your shrine do so in a respectful way, bowing to the Buddha. Make sure you keep your shrine clean and tidy. You might want to do your daily practice in front of your shrine, or offer incense once a day, or do three prostrations.

Something else that is nice to do is carrying a 'portable shrine' around with you when you go on holiday or travel – a small Buddha and a candle will suffice. In this way you will always be accompanied wherever you go.

Making offerings
Satyavani

Making offerings at the shrine is a way of showing respect to the Buddha, and of showing our gratitude for the three jewels. It's a bit like wanting your guest to eat your best food and stay in a room which has beautiful things in it.

There are a number of traditional offerings – fresh flowers in a vase, incense, food, something to represent music, water and candles or other lights. Some shrines have two bowls of water –representing water to drink and to wash with. If you don't have an incense holder you can fill a bowl with rice and use this to hold the burning incense.

Arrange your offerings around the Buddha artfully, and maybe keep spare incense and a box of matches underneath the shrine. You might want to buy a singing bowl to ring before and after meditation too.

When you offer incense you can recite an offering verse, maybe eventually learning one or two off by heart. You can find these in the *Meal time and incense offerings* chapter.

You can also make a water offering by pouring some water from a jug into two or three small bowls set in front of the Buddha, and then lifting these up high one by one. When you change the water make sure the blessed water goes into a plant or into the garden onto a living thing so that none of the blessings are lost.

Nei quan and chi quan

Kaspalita

Nei quan is the practice of getting to know the human condition and our own human nature particularly. Chih quan is the practice of bringing our own particular human nature with all of its flaws and rough edges into relationship with the Buddha. Through these practices, we deepen our experience of the nembutsu, the act of connecting ourselves as ordinary foolish beings to the Buddha.

> Nei Quan and Chih Quan are ancillary. All is already there within the nembutsu, but these spiritual exercises help us to appreciate it and open the gateway to simplicity. They do not provide intellectual understanding, but they provide the opportunity for us to feel the nembutsu in our flesh, bone and marrow. Thus is the Buddhist life lived and its fruit known in direct experience. Thus we practise faith and find faith in practice through experience.[35]

In this practice we are not aiming to change what we are, but to be at peace with it.

---

[35] Brazier, David *Instructions in Nei Quan and Chih Quan* http://lotusinthemud.typepad.com/amida_groups/2011/11/instructions-in-nei-quan-and-chih-quan.html accessed 3/11/15

Nei quan comes from two Chinese characters that mean 'looking deeply' or 'looking beneath the surface.' We practise nei quan in different ways in this community, from the formal naikan practice created by Yoshimoto Ishin in Japan in the 20th century to more organic and associative ways of looking into our own hearts. Other investigative Buddhist practices, like vipassana, can also been seen as a kind of nei quan.

Earlier this year, Dharmavidya led a nei quan sesshin at his place in France. Sesshin is a Japanese word that means to look into one's heart – so this was a retreat to look deeply into our own hearts.

On the first day of the retreat, after morning service in the barn and breakfast beneath the vast walnut tree, we made our way up to the attic room. We sat there beneath the exposed oak roof beams, on comfortable arm chairs and sofas and Dharmavidya introduced the practice for the retreat.

The retreat had four different elements: Practice in the shrine room, where we would chant nembutsu and practise chih quan, bringing ourselves into a closer relationship to Amida; instruction by Dharmavidya; the nei quan investigation; and making reports of our progress. Some of the practices and advice I'll refer to here were given by Dharmavidya during the instruction on this retreat.

For the nei quan investigation we were asked to look deeply into our own hearts. (In Buddhism the word for 'heart' and 'mind' is often the same – you can think of 'heart/mind' whenever you see 'heart' or 'mind' in English writings about Buddhism.) The aim was to see what was really there, and then to look deeper. Dharmavidya used the image of many different boxes as a metaphor for what we would find in the investigation. We open one box and look into it. What we find is many other boxes. This is not a process of getting to the end of something, but of learning what the many parts of ourselves are, and learning something about human nature along the way.

We wrote in our journals throughout the retreat as a way of assisting this process. My own experience of journaling is that writing gives me access to parts of myself that merely thinking does not. I found having a paper and pen a great help.

At least once a day we had the opportunity to make a report. This is a feature of naikan as practised on retreat in Japan. When you give a report in a naikan retreat it is done in a voice loud enough for others to hear. Other people may be prompted by things they hear in your report, 'oh yes, that applies to me as well' or 'that reminds me of...'. The report is also a chance for the retreat leader (or one of their assistants on the large Japanese retreats) to redirect your investigation if need be, or simply encourage you to keep going. Usually you will just be thanked for giving your report.

The act of being witnessed and having your report accepted is a powerful one. In the nei quan retreat in France we were invited to come into the centre of the space and sit opposite Dharmavidya. We would bow to him, as our teacher and the retreat leader, and he would bow back to us, and then we would give our report.

I felt that whatever I had to offer in these reports was accepted by Dharmavidya. In those moments he was a Buddha for me. His being at peace with what I talked about, whatever I had found in my heart, moved me closer towards finding peace with it myself.

If we are practising nei quan on our own away from a retreat setting, it's important to also practise chih quan and have a sense of being accepted by the Buddha.

Listening to the reports of others that week not only gave me ideas for my own investigations into myself, but led me to a tender feeling towards each of the other participants. As we go through daily life and people push our buttons, it can be easy to forget that everyone has hidden depths. We are all scarred in some way. The retreat space and the reporting process allowed each person to become vulnerable and expose some of their scars and open wounds, and when I really listened to their experience I felt a great sense of kindliness towards each person.

Tips for your nei quan practice

Be Specific

We have a tendency to make generalisations: to make things more simple than they are. There is a value in this, but we frequently make the wrong generalisation, preferring something that fits with our idea of who we are and what the world is like, rather than examining the evidence first and then making a generalisation. Examining the evidence may challenge our ideas about ourselves and the world, but it is this that will lead to liberation.

From a Pureland Buddhist point of view, I expect that when you examine the evidence the kind of generalisations you will come up with will be something about the universality of bombu nature. There are some things we can overcome, but as well as the seeds of compassion and fellow feeling we all have the seeds of greed, hate and delusion and we often let them flower.

Look for the Clinging

When I practise nei quan informally away from the shrine room or retreat space I often find that I am looking for the conceit. In the year before moving into the temple there were times when I felt particularly challenged; moving house is often talked about as one of the most stressful things one can do. Not only was I moving house, I was also moving the home of our local Sangha, finding tenants for my old house and trying to influence the buying process over which I had no control (that was between the trustees and the solicitors of the various other parties). There were many times during that process when my buttons were pushed and I could feel an unhelpful energy rising up in me. Sometimes I caught it as the energy was rising, and sometimes I reflected on the feelings after they had led me to unskilful action, or had simply become locked into my body as tension in my neck and shoulders.

In those moments, or after those moments, I would take myself to a quiet space and look into my own heart. I was looking for the selfishness, or the fear. In my experience whenever anger or upset arises there is always some selfish core. Usually the energy comes up in order to protect some aspect of my identity, or view of the world, that I am clinging to when it is no longer true or useful.

If I could find the story that I was clinging to and bring it to the Buddha, I would feel the tension beginning to dissipate, and have a sense of being accepted just as I was. Sometimes it was just enough to see the story, sometimes it was helpful to look further and ask where that story had come from and why I was holding on to it.

As I brought those parts of myself into relationship with the Buddha, they began to lose the dysfunctional hold over me. I could either let them go, or bring that energy into the service of the Buddha.

Turn it around

If you are practising nei quan in your journal or just looking into your heart, there are some questions you can ask yourself which may help reveal what has been hidden:

- If this is true, when is the opposite true?
- If I am afraid of X is that because I give X? Or is there part of me that invites it?
- If I am angry about X in someone else, where is X in me?

We are looking for what is true, and if we see ourselves thinking 'I am like this' or 'I am like that' we should be wary, because we are never always just one thing. If we think 'I am the sort of person who…' we should ask 'When am I not this person?'

For example if we notice we are angry, or feel like an angry person we can ask ourselves:

What triggers my anger?
When does it increase?
When does it fade?
When am I not angry?
Are there times when it is appropriate? And so on.

236

Naikan

Yoshimoto Ishin created naikan based on his experience of working therapeutically with people in prison. He noticed that there were common stories amongst the prisoners that were not true, but that they would cling on to. In response to this he created the naikan meditation – a series of questions for the prisoners to reflect upon that would disrupt those stories and bring them closer to the truth of their own lives.

The three questions are:

1. What have I received?
2. What have I offered in return?
3. What trouble has my existence caused?

The practice worked so well that it spread beyond prisons, and there are now around 50 naikan retreat centres in Japan where you can go and be led through a whole week or more of working with these questions.

The naikan halls in these retreat centres tend to be very beautiful and each person's space is separated form the next one by a paper screen. You have a sense of the people around you and can hear their reports, but you are also protected from the distraction of seeing them directly.

Throughout the course of the retreat, the *naikansha* (retreat leader) will usually take you through a process of reviewing your whole life using these three questions. For example on the first day you might be asked to explore the relationship between yourself as an infant and your primary care giver: What did I receive from my primary care giver? What did I do in return? What trouble did my existence cause them?

The naikan practice is aimed at showing you the truth. You may have an experience of seeing that you received a great deal and feel grateful about that. Or you may realise that you received very little, and grieve for that. In any case, you must have received enough to have survived and even if it was very little it may still have cost your care giver a great deal to give even this much, given their own circumstances. It is a practice of coming to terms with what is true.

As well as the more organic, exploratory form of nei quan described above, we can use these naikan prompts in our own practice.

When I lived in The Buddhist House we usually had time each morning using these questions. We would use them to examine the last 24 hours, or the time since we had last practised (if we had not had any reflection time over a weekend, for example).

I am sure that regularly doing this practice changed how I saw the world. I became interested in the impact I was having upon the world and in other people's experience of me. I moved towards a more authentic sense of myself in the world.

Practised on its own, naikan can be quite confronting. It can reveal unexpected truths that we might previously have shied away from. When we practised in The Buddhist House it was always paired with chih quan, and I am sure this second practice made the naikan possible and the truths easier to come to terms with.

Chih quan

Chih and quan are the Chinese characters for peaceful meditation and in our tradition we practise this by making offerings to Amida Buddha. Whatever we discover in our hearts, whatever the answers to the naikan prompts are, whatever is arising in us, we hand it over to the Buddha. You might have a visual sense of doing this in your imagination, or just a felt sense of the Buddha's presence which you can pass things to. If you can really present what you have discovered to the Buddha, he will accept it completely. Everything that is in your heart is loveable, to the Buddha, just as it is. Sometimes we will have an experience of feeling accepted that is very powerful. Other times we just trust that it is the case, and this trust can be enough for us to begin the process of accepting for ourselves what is in our own hearts.

As we come to see what is in our own hearts more clearly, all of the loving impulses and all of the selfish impulses, and have a sense that all of those are acceptable and lovable, it becomes easier for us to trust that the same is true for other people too. Even if we cannot always accept all the different parts of the people we find ourselves in relationship with, we can trust that the Buddha will be able to, and this can be enough to bring a new sense of ease to these relationships and undermine our own defensive reflexes.

Dharmavidya encourages us to understand the peace that we experience in chih quan as Amida Buddha. This peace is the experience of Amida Buddha entering into us. Thus nei quan and chih quan together give us an experience of the nembutsu. In nei quan we understand 'Namo', we understand who and what calls out. In chih quan we understand 'Amida Bu', we experience the Buddha that we are calling to. It is in this sense that nei quan and chih quan are auxiliary practices, adding depth of meaning to the primary practice, which is the nembutsu itself. In nei quan we explore what it really means to be human – what is the exact nature of our bombu nature – and in chih quan we bring all of that to the Buddha, and feel loved, just as we are.

Prostrations

Satyavani

When I first attended Buddhist services in the Buddhist House, the bit that made me the most uncomfortable was when everyone made a semi-circle around the Buddha and, after kneeling, dropped forward to put their foreheads on the carpet. I copied them as they lifted their forearms above their heads, palms up. My face was burning, and I felt like I wanted to bolt from the room.

When I moved to Malvern with Kaspa and we started holding services in our tiny living room (which looked out onto the street), I remember feeling embarrassed that passers-by might look in and see us prostrating. Even the word 'prostrate' left me feeling unsettled. It either reminded me of prostate cancer or conjured a kind of naked helplessness I didn't want to dwell on.

Bowing can be particularly challenging for Westerners. Our culture tells us that we should be self-sufficient, and that we shouldn't put ourselves below anyone else where we will be vulnerable. Judith Lief says:

> As Westerners we tend to think of prostrating as a gesture of defeat or abasement. We think that to show someone else respect is to make ourselves less. Prostrating irritates our sense of democracy, that everyone is equal....

241

On one hand we want to receive the teachings but on the other we don't really want to bow down to anyone or anything.[36]

Of course, a feeling of naked helplessness is the whole point of prostrations. When we lie flat on our bellies in front of the Buddha we are exposing the back of our necks, which was a traditional way of showing strangers that we trusted them. If they wanted to they could easily slice into our neck with their sword, and that would be the end of us.

I have to make an effort now to remember how it felt to do prostrations back then as prostrations are probably my favourite practice now. There is something about resting my forehead on the ground that is a great relief – I can let go of all my self-importance and efforts to be in control, and relax on the ground with the Buddha above me, just where he should be. Sometimes when I am doing prostrations alone I will linger on the floor, not wanting to get up, feeling the muscles in my back relaxing bit by bit.

Bowing and prostrations can be found in all the world's religious traditions, and the practice has a variety of different functions or effects. We bow to each other as a social courtesy, or as a form of repentance. We prostrate to deities to establish a worshipful relationship with them, or to say thank you to them. We bow to increase our humility and to decrease our ego. We bow because we belong on the floor. We let ourselves down onto the floor and we feel Mother Earth support us

Bowing and full prostrations are used in various ways in Pureland Buddhism. In our school we do a set of five full

---

[36] Lief, Judith *Bowing* Tricycle (Fall 1994)

prostrations during morning and evening service – the first prostration to Amida, then the Buddha, Dharma, Sangha and Pure Land. We also bow a lot both during formal practice and elsewhere – if in doubt, bow! During formal practice we bow to our seats in the shrine room to show respect, we bow to ask permission to enter the sacred space around the shrine, we bow to each other, we bow to the room when we enter or exit, we bow after meditating or to the Celebrant to say thank you for the Dharma talk. In less formal situations we bow after we bless the food, to visitors when we greet them, or to each other. I like to bow to our big Buddha in the garden alcove whenever I pass him (although if I bowed to every Buddha in the temple when I walked past I'd never get anywhere very quickly!). A bow is a bit like saying the nembutsu – it puts us into relationship with the Buddhas, and it reminds us of our position in relation to the infinite – how small and limited we are, and how grateful we can be for all the things we receive.

Try one out right now. Put your hands together in the *gassho* (Japanese) or *anjali* (Sanskirt) mudra, as if you are praying, with your hands upright and palms together at chest level. Bow at the waist – don't bow in a perfunctory way, bow as if you mean it. I am bowing back.

Breathing nembutsu
Satyavani

I was told about this practice by Rob, one of our Australian Sangha members. One of its advantages is that you can do it anywhere – on a busy train, sitting in your living room while other people are watching television, or in the middle of the night when you wake up and feel frightened for no discernable reason.

To do the practice you imagine the words of the nembutsu accompanying your breath as it naturally rises and falls. During the in-breath you imagine the words 'Namo A-' and during the out-breath you imagine '-mida Bu'. Don't try to alter the length of your breath – some breaths will be short or shallow, some will be longer. Just allow the nembutsu to follow your breath as a cork would bob up and down on gentle waves.

As you continue, see if you can allow the nembutsu to become more and more fluid. There may be a natural pause on the first 'a' of Amida as your breath pauses between coming in and going out again. There will also be a complete break after the 'Bu' as your body pauses before taking in another breath. Allow these pauses to be there.

Sometimes the nembutsu I hear has a tune – the tune of the chant we use for our prostrations. Sometimes it doesn't. Sometimes I imagine a golden glow accompanying the chant, or the presence of Amida Buddha. You can experiment and see what feels right for you. It doesn't matter too much though. As with all spiritual practice we're not looking for 'results' like feeling calmer or feeling more connected to the Buddha (although these will often be happy by-products). We are simply bringing ourselves into relationship with something bigger than ourselves and trusting that this will be a helpful thing to do in the long run.

The breathing nembutsu also works well if you are doing a period of quiet sitting. Sit upright in your usual meditation posture on a zafu or on a chair and allow the nembutsu to follow your breath. When you get distracted (you will!) simply bring your attention back to the nembutsu. You could set yourself a timer on your phone and do five or fifteen minutes, or simply sit for as long as you feel is good for you to sit.

Continuous nembutsu
Satyavani

One of my favourite Pureland practices is the continuous nembutsu. I try to make sure we have a chanting day scheduled around the time of my birthday as a day of chanting with friends followed by a curry in Vasai, our local Indian, is the best way I can think of celebrating.

During the continuous nembutsu, the chant carries on in the shrine room for the duration of the practice. Sometimes we do six hours, sometimes twenty four, and one year at The Buddhist House they were crazy enough to do ten days and nights in a row!

The chant takes the same form as the chant we do at the beginning of service and is accompanied by the mokugyo. The drum is hit with a wooden mallet four times, 'donk donk donk donk', and then the chanting starts:

Namo Ami- da Bu Namo Ami- da Bu etc.
donk donk donk donk donk donk etc.

The mokugyo keeps us in time and adds some percussion to the chanting when we are sitting down. The room generally divides into two teams – one team chants 'Namo Amida Bu' four times then pauses for two, and the other does the same but overlapping with the other team by one nembutsu at each end.

This means that the chant never stops and that we can all breathe!

We sit for twenty minutes, walk slowly around the shrine for twenty minutes (still chanting), sit for twenty minutes and so on. The chant begins on one note but as time goes on little slides up and down are introduced and become exaggerated – by the end of the first hour we are usually chanting in a tune, sometimes with several harmonies. Sometimes the chant is in a minor key and sometimes major, sometimes it is lively and sometimes elegiac, sometimes it is tuneful and sometimes not!

As the day progresses, different people appear and join in the walking or sitting. Others leave to have a cup of tea, eat in the room next door, or to go home. It's lovely to see old friends appearing at the door – some who've travelled quite some way to join in, and to hear their familiar voices blending with the others. It's also lovely to see new faces – people who've never been to the temple before – and to see them gradually relax into the practice.

Chanting in this way can be a challenging practice for some people to begin with. Chanting isn't something we're used to doing in this country, and people sometimes feel self-conscious at the sound of their own voice and worried about getting it 'wrong'. Combine this with the unfamiliar etiquette of the shrine room and people can feel very outside of their comfort zone. Generally if they stay long enough they relax into the chanting and forget about what people might be thinking of them. As their voices grow a little louder and they remember to bow when the bell rings, they blend into the group and it can feel like we know them without having shared a single word with them.

The continuous nembutsu practice has a knack of showing you yourself like a very wise mirror. One of the things I used to struggle with a lot was not being in control of what happens in the room. When you are on your own or when you are Celebrant you can change the pitch or speed of the chant at will. When there are five or ten of you, you can try and speed things up or slow things down, but if the room doesn't want to do that, they won't obey! The chant really does take on a life of its own, and after many days of continuous nembutsu I am beginning to get the message. I notice anxiety coming up when things aren't going how I think they should be going (maybe the chant is out of tune or a new person doesn't seem to be relaxing into it). I notice the impulse to try and 'make it better' – chanting more loudly so others are bullied into copying me, or smiling too much at the new person. I return to the chanting and feel the anxiety gradually ebbing away. Sometimes this pattern is repeated many times before I finally surrender to the group, stop worrying about others, and put my focus back onto the chanting and the Buddha where it belongs.

Different people experience different things during the chanting. Some feel annoyed by the sound of someone else breathing or feel driven to distraction by how fidgety they feel when we sit for twenty minutes. Others think it all seems a bit silly. We are all unique and we all see ourselves reflected back in unique ways in the mirror of the chanting. We can learn a lot about ourselves on these days, often things we'd rather not have known.

The chanting has a very different effect on different people. Some people find that, within the container of the nembutsu and the people present, difficult emotions bubble up and spill over. One new member, who was an experienced

Buddhist practitioner in a different school, said that he was surprised about how emotional he found the experience, and that as he chanted sadness rose up from nowhere. Someone else reported remembering painful childhood memories, and found it difficult to stay in the shrine room for a while. Sometimes people feel spaced out with bliss or deeply calm, sometimes they feel a bit embarrassed, and sometimes they feel nothing at all.

I often find the experience of chanting quite mundane – I think about having a cup of tea in ten minutes, or some job I have to do tomorrow, or my mind just goes blank. As the years have gone on, I do feel more joy during the chanting, and feel more settled in it – the time seems to whoosh by in a way that it rarely did when I first attended the practice and five minutes could last forever. It's often towards the end of the day or later that the effects of the practice catch up with me. I find myself being overwhelmed with gratitude at someone new arriving, or by looking at the smile on the Buddha's face. Tears often come at this point and I have to stop chanting until my voice stops catching. I also feel an 'after-effect' of the chanting over the next days and weeks – I feel more stable, more grounded, and more in touch with the beauty of the world.

Once when we were chanting in a beautiful Quaker meeting house, Howard was struggling with his health and he lay down on some cushions at the back where he chanted or just listened. As I walked round I remember feeling great gratitude for the fact that he was resting for me, and that I was keeping on walking and chanting for him. It was as if we had become one person and so it was possible for me to both rest and to chant – I didn't have to do it all. This is Sangha as refuge.

Whatever we feel or don't feel during the chanting, we do it because we have faith that it is a good thing to do. If we are in relationship with a teacher from the Amida-shu school then we do it because we trust our teacher – just as Shinran Shonen said that he would follow his teacher, Honen, to hell if that's what he asked him to do. We might do it because we know someone in the Sangha who seems to get something good from coming, and so we see if we can get something too. We might do it because it's what Pureland Buddhists have been doing for hundreds of years. This faith carries us through and means that we don't have to be sure that we are 'getting something' in return for our time or energy or money. The transactional/commercial model doesn't suit spiritual practice, but it's the one most of us have been brought up with and so it can feel odd to do something that doesn't seem to make any sense or that we can't describe to other people. Notice these thoughts when they come up and let them go. Just carry on chanting.

After such long periods of hearing the same phrase over and over, the chant can stay with you. After our most recent eleven hour chant (Kaspa, Jnanamati and I chanted for about ten hours, once you take away time for eating, going to the toilet etc.) I lay in bed that night and literally listened to a choir quietly singing Namo Amida Bu in my head. It wasn't that I was imagining it – I could hear the voices as if they were outside of me. You could make sense of this as some of my brain cells getting stuck on a loop, or you could see it as a spiritual experience. It doesn't matter – either way it was a lovely thing to listen to as I went to sleep.

Continuous chanting is special as it gives us a more immersive experience of chanting and of hearing the nembutsu. It brings us together with others from our

Sangha, and it shows us how we are bombu beings in relationship with Amida Buddha. We're not in control of very much – all we can do is say the name of Amida and trust that we will be looked after. Continuous chanting shows us that we can trust – the chant goes faster or slower depending on what the group needs, and people show up with delicious food to keep us nourished and with smiles or a wink to revive us when we need reviving at three o'clock in the afternoon when we're feeling sleepy and bored. We let go into the group and we know that we will be held – by each other, by the sacred space, and by the golden Buddha, who watches us for hour after hour and who is pleased that we are there with him.

Listening circle
Satyavani

As we have said one of the important practices we have in our tradition is the listening circle or stone passing. We have both already spoken about why we feel these spaces are important, and told stories about our own experience in these circles. What follows is a list of instructions and suggestions if you'd like to hold your own listening circle.

When holding listening circles it is, if possible, helpful to have at least one person present who has had experience of this kind of sharing before and who feels comfortable holding the space and modelling both listening and sharing from the heart. The more experienced people present, the more grounded the space will feel. You don't have to worry too much as the group will tend to unconsciously limit the depth of their sharing if the group is newer or feels more nervous or tentative. As you continue to meet and as faith grows, you may find people sharing emotion more often, or that they are able to be more vulnerable.

It may occasionally be necessary to hold a boundary. In the listening circle the boundaries will be both explicit and implicit, and delineate the specific culture that makes the space safer than most spaces. These explicit and implicit rules might include starting and finishing on time, people turning off their phones, everyone listening carefully to each other, and the use of a room where the group won't be interrupted. An example of a boundary breach is if someone starts speaking when someone else is holding the stone. It is important for those speaking to know that they can speak without anyone else responding, and so if others interrupt and they're not gently corrected it potentially leaves the whole group feeling unsure about whether or not this will happen to them as well.

If the group is more experienced, group members may share their thoughts and feelings about other people who are present in the group – e.g. if they have appreciated something they shared earlier, or if they have had a difficult interaction elsewhere which is unresolved. They might choose to give the stone to the person they've shared about, who can then hold the stone and respond to what's been said, and the stone can be 'swapped back and forth' a few times until the issue has been resolved (or at least aired).

If you have new people attending the circle (as we do here at the temple) it may be helpful to read some guidelines out at the beginning of the hour. I have copied ours below which you might want to use or adapt.

Once the allocated time is up, or if everyone has said what they want to say and there is a period of silence when no-one picks up the stone again, we like to finish with a verse. In Malvern we have both Buddhists and non-Buddhists attending, and so we use a verse which Kaspa adapted from the Sussusa Sutta:

We have listened to each other. We have opened our ears. We have opened our hearts and minds to receive wisdom. We have taken what is worthwhile

254

and not taken what is not. With patience we will take what we have received into our lives.

We bow in gratitude.

If you are doing the listening circle in a more Amidist setting (as we do after our services once a month on a Wednesday night) it is traditional to finish with the original and sacred vows:

> The original and sacred vows
> are the unique and essential grace
> by which to enter the Pure Land.
> Therefore with body, speech and mind
> we are devoted to the teachings
> that all may attain the state of bliss.

After we've spoken one of these verses in unison we stand and bow to each other (into the centre of the circle) as a way of showing our gratitude and respect for each other, and then to the Buddha (in the direction of the Buddha statue or the shrine in the room).

You might want to hold listening circles as part of a retreat day, after a service (we finish our weekly Wednesday service once a month with a listening circle for half an hour) or on its own (we have one every Sunday evening). Remind people that listening is the most important part, remember that the circle is held by Amida, and enjoy the deepening of truth, connection and faith that this practice will bring.

Listening circle guidelines

To be read out at the start of each meeting

- We finish at 7.30pm or earlier.
- Please keep everything you hear confidential.
- When someone has the stone, everyone else is quiet and listens.
- When you are handed the stone, introduce yourself and then say what is in your heart. You can be quiet if you prefer.
- You can refer to what others have said, but we generally don't give advice. Instead we learn by listening to others speaking from their own experience.
- If it is a big group, please be conscious of how long you speak for.
- When you are finished speaking, hand the stone to someone who hasn't yet spoken.
- If you are the last person to speak, put the stone in the centre. Anyone who wants to speak again can take it and put it back again afterwards.
- Some of the group are Pureland Buddhists and say 'Namo Amida Bu', a way of connecting with Amida Buddha. Feel free to say this too, or not. If you have any questions do ask afterwards.
- The toilet is at the top of the stairs.
- Feel free to attend every week or every so often. Do bring others – all are welcome.
- We suggest a donation of £5 or whatever you can afford to support the temple. The donation bowl is in the hallway.

A simple daily practice
Satyavani

If you want to practise in the Amida-shu all you need to do is say Namo Amida Bu. Having said this, most of us benefit from a more formalised and regular period of practice where we put our worldly concerns aside and spend some 'quality' time with the Buddha. These routines and rituals are seen as 'auxiliary practices' in our tradition – simply saying the nembutsu is sufficient – but they can be helpful to practitioners in strengthening their connection with the Buddha and each other and deepening their experience of refuge. They often have happy side-effects as we feel calmer or more full of joy during or after practice, or have an insight into something that has been troubling us. They can also be seen as a celebration of the blessings we already receive from the Buddhas.

It is helpful to establish a particular place for your practice as this place will build up good associations: after practising there for some time, you may find that as soon as you enter the area you feel different. This doesn't need to be grand – a zafu on the piece of floor next to the bookcase with your shrine on will suffice, or a corner of your bedroom where you can put a chair and a small table with a Buddha statue on it. If practical, any statue of Shakyamuni Buddha that you have should face west towards the Pure Land, and Amida Buddha should face east, sitting in the Pureland.

What you choose to include in your daily (or less than daily!) practice is personal choice. You can choose from different chants, walking meditation, sitting meditation, reciting liturgy from the *Nien Fo Book*, prostrations, listening to Dharma talks or making offerings to the shrine. My suggestion would be that to start with you keep it simple. When Kaspa started practising he'd just do three prostrations in front of the shrine every morning, and recently he's been offering incense to his Buddha at the start of every work day. When I first started practising on my own I'd sit and chant along to some recorded chants on the Friends of Amida website for five minutes, and then sit quietly for five minutes. What you do is less important than the spirit with which you do it – be respectful and take the practice seriously, but also keep a light touch, allowing feelings of joy and gratitude to arise when they are there.

Dharmavidya has here suggested a short formal service for beginners that you can follow at home either on your own or with a friend:

> Enter your shrine area and stand facing the Buddha. Make five prostrations, saying nembutsu to yourself as you do so. Then sit in front of your shrine and ensure that it is clean and tidy. You may want to make new offerings of clean water or fruit, making additional bows as you do so. Keep your mind in a reverent attitude throughout. Sit in meditation for ten minutes, contemplating the Pure Land, then recite the Sevenfold Prayer. Stand up. Bow to anybody else who is practising with you. Bow to the Buddha. Straighten your seat and make your sitting area tidy before you leave. Say the nembutsu as you

depart. Later you will be able to sit for longer, include other texts, add some walking meditation and vary the practice as you learn more.

The Sevenfold Prayer is as follows:

> With body, speech, and mind, humbly I prostrate,
> And make offerings both set out and imagined.
> I confess my wrong deeds from all time,
> And rejoice in the virtues of all.
> Please stay until samsara ceases,
> And turn the Wheel of Dharma for us.
> I dedicate all virtues to great enlightenment.

Other things practitioners might begin to include in their daily routine are: reciting the *Summary of Faith and Practice* (see appendix D); doing walking meditation outside; using a mala, a Buddhist set of prayer beads used to count recitations; doing nei quan and chih quan or reciting other texts from the *Nien Fo Book* or the *Larger Pureland Sutra*. Amida-shu isn't the kind of Sangha which decides centrally how people should practise. As individuals we are encouraged to be creative and find our own way with our practice, supported by more experienced practitioners. As groups we are encouraged to find out what works in our locality, and to meet the particular needs of the group whilst drawing on the common forms of practice within Amida-shu and following the spirit of the nembutsu.

It is traditional to end formal practice sessions by reciting this verse (usually the first one people learn by heart):

The original and sacred vows
Are the unique and essential grace
By which to enter the Pure Land.
Therefore, with body, speech and mind
We are devoted to the teachings
That all may attain the state of bliss.

When we can it is important for us to do longer periods of practice both alone (for example by taking a whole day to alternate between writing in our journals and sitting quietly) and with other Sangha members (perhaps an all-day chanting day or a retreat day). This gives our practice a 'boost' and allows us to slowly settle into a more contemplative state of mind with the practice becoming a container where we can seek refuge. If no Amida-shu events are available, you could attend other Buddhist or even other religion's retreat days. I have found great spiritual solace in Cathedrals and once at a Carmelite monastery. We should be careful that we don't become precious about 'our practice' – it is possible to join in with other's spiritual practices and see these as a form of nembutsu, or as another formal way of connecting with the divine/the Buddha.

Finally, we can say the nembutsu throughout the day, whenever we remember. Sometimes I like to chant when I'm driving, either using a tune or just speaking the words quickly or slowly. We can say 'Namo Amida Bu' when we greet and say goodbye to members of the Sangha, before we eat as a quick grace, when something goes well or when something goes badly. In this way we are continually turning ourselves towards the light of Amida, either consciously or unconsciously, and resting in the knowledge that we will be held by the Buddhas, whatever happens.

Pureland Buddhist services and ceremonies
Satyavani

When groups of Amida-shu Buddhists meet at the temple or in their homes we practise together by following a formal programme which lasts about an hour. These programmes are known as services. They usually consist of a mixture of chanting, sitting and walking nembutsu, a short Dharma talk, prostrations and liturgy. All the liturgy can be found in the *Nien Fo Book* which is available online.[37] There are different formats of practice for morning, afternoon and evening service. Here in Malvern we have an evening service at 7.30 p.m. on Wednesdays, a morning service at 8 a.m. on Fridays, and an adapted form of the afternoon service at 10 a.m. on Sundays.

Our morning service starts with the congregation seated in the shrine room quietly. At five minutes before eight the bellmaster rings a gong to summon everyone to service. At 8 a.m. someone starts striking the mokugyo, the wooden fish that we use during continuous chanting retreats, and the congregation chant 'Namo Amida Bu' until the celebrant enters. This vigorous practice is meant to 'rouse us' to concentrate on the practice to follow and to sound throughout the temple, inviting the celebrant and attendants

---

[37] http://amidatrust.ning.com/page/useful-texts

to appear. The celebrant will make offerings to the shrine, pouring water into the offering pots and maybe lighting some incense. We then join together in circumambulating the shrine as we chant 'Namo Omito Fo', the Chinese form of Namo Amida Bu. After ten or fifteen minutes the bellmaster rings her inkin once which tells us all to return to our seats, and the chant finishes with another ring of the inkin and a bow. We then recite the *Summary of Faith and Practice* together before sitting for some formal meditation. Afterwards we gather around the shrine to recite the morning liturgy together (a mixture of chanting and reading), followed by five prostrations accompanied by the prostrations chant. There will then be a Dharma talk by the celebrant, and we all bow to each other and the Buddha before an incense offering is made and we all exit silently. The ordained people leave first in order of seniority and are followed by the rest of the congregation.

During services we all take care to show our respect to the Buddha, the shrine room and each other. For example, when someone comes in at the beginning and sits opposite us we make gassho to them, and we bow to our seat at the end of service to thank it for supporting us. We tune into each other by taking our lead from the celebrant, and moving more quietly and gracefully than we might elsewhere. The atmosphere that builds is one of solemn reverence and quiet contemplation sometimes punctured by an occasional lighter moment if the bellmaster laughs at themselves for making a mistake, or if the celebrant makes a joke during their Dharma talk. I sometimes say to newcomers who are worried about 'getting it wrong' that if in doubt they should bow!

There are many advantages to following a more formalised structure when practising together. One is that it joins the Sangha together – both between groups and within groups. We know that Amida-shu groups across the world are reading the same verses and chanting the same liturgy. We also join our voices together in our local groups as we read the *Summary of Faith and Practice* in unison, or chant the evening chant 'Amitabha' as we circumambulate the Buddha. We become familiar with the various elements of service, and they engrave the nembutsu more deeply into our hearts, like repeated readings of a favourite poem. A more formal mode of practice reminds us (or helps newcomers to discover) how important it is that we put the Buddha in the centre of our lives.

My own experience of attending service regularly is that it is often a doorway into gratitude, peace, and a tangible feeling of being closer to the Buddha. This isn't always the case – sometimes I spend Friday morning wishing I'd eaten some breakfast first, or wondering if the sitting meditation will ever end. Practice isn't a shortcut to bliss, or a method by which we become perfect human beings, but as we bring ourselves into relationship with the Buddha his qualities really do start rubbing off on us, bit by bit. It is often the place where I receive insights about myself and others, either in meditation or whilst walking and chanting, or whilst listening to the Dharma talk. It is also the place where I tend to have what I'd categorise as spiritual experiences: sudden whooshes of gratitude, fellow feeling and intimacy with all things that bring me to tears. These might happen as I watch a blackbird balancing on the railing outside the big window behind the Buddha, or as I listen to us all as we walk and chant Amida's name. Service is where Quan Yin Bodhisattva visits me, and where I am able to peel off thin layers of ego one by one and discard them on the floor behind me. Service is where the light gets in.

Here at the temple we follow most of our services with a cup of tea and a biscuit in the dining room which is next door to the shrine room. This gives people a chance to get to know each other and to ask any questions they might have about the service, or about Buddhism in general. On Sundays, we often follow this cup of tea with a couple of hours work cleaning the house or in the temple garden for anyone who wants to stay and help out. Working together is a crucial part of Sangha building and when someone comes to their second service I often ask them to wash up the mugs after service as their initiation and welcome into the group. As Buddhists we are learning how to be of service to our Sangha and local community and ultimately to all sentient beings. We can start by polishing the mirror in the shrine room!

Different groups around the country will use different formats for their meetings, as you'll see in the chapter on forming your own Pureland practice group. For instance, some regularly include a study section on an extract from a Buddhist book, or a bring and share meal. The important thing is that we are gathering together to say the name of Amida Buddha, and sharing this practice with each other – that person we've just fallen out with, those people who have really been irritating us, or that person we are desperate to impress. We turn up as we are, with our current preoccupations and anxieties, and with our self-importance and our self-doubt. As we practise we hand all this over to the Buddha and trust that the nembutsu is working on us, often despite our unconscious attempts to sabotage it and to cling onto our egos. Little by little, we are transformed under the loving gaze of the Buddha. We let go of our fear. We become Buddhas practising with other Buddhas. We luxuriate in this love. And then, more importantly than anything else, we take this love out into our daily lives and we offer it to others.

Appendices

Appendix A: How to start your own Pureland Buddhist group

Satyavani

There really is no substitute for sharing our spiritual journey with friends, practising together and coming together in community. Sangha is the third jewel. At this point there are only a scattering of Amida-shu Buddhist groups around the world. If you are interested in Amida-shu Buddhism, where can you find your Sangha?

If you can, we'd recommend that you link up with an existing Amida-shu Sangha – come to stay at the temple in Malvern, or attend a retreat day in Belgium or Canada or elsewhere. Even visiting once a year can make a big difference to daily practice. We also have an online community which is helpful for those who are geographically isolated or who feel comfortable relating to others online.[38] We offer a couple of online study programmes which are a good way of getting to know others from the Sangha, and if you contact us we may be able to put you in touch with other Amida-shu members in your area.

It may support your practice to attend other Pureland Buddhist groups. There are Jodo Shinshu temples in the UK, for example, and in America Nishi-Hongwanji (the biggest

---

[38] www.amidatrust.ning.com

Jodo Shinshu organisation in Japan) have established the Buddhist Churches of America. Of course there are also many other forms of Buddhism with groups and temples in the West – go and visit a couple and see what feels right. We don't just find Dharma and Sangha in Buddhist circles either. I have personally learnt a great deal in recent years from Christian writings about prayer and about having a personal relationship with God. I've had many helpful conversations with people of other faiths, and we've shared moments of deep affinity and understanding.

Another option is to create your own Pureland practice group in the style of Amida-shu. This isn't as daunting as it sounds. To begin with it might just be two or three of you who meet once a month to swap notes on the online Introductory Course, to do some chanting together, or to read from one of Dharmavidya's books.

In the Amida Sangha there are no set rules for how groups operate. Each group needs to find a way of meeting the local requirements of the group and this will depend on who starts the group, the culture of the local area, recent history and other factors. The important golden thread is our core practice as Pureland Buddhists, and the warm and welcoming spirit of Amida-shu which runs through all of our groups in one way or another. Dharmavidya says: 'Each local group ... is encouraged to be creative and to find what works best for them within some broad parameters, or, more properly, within the spirit of the nembutsu.'[39]

---

39 Brazier, David http://lotusinthemud.typepad.com/amida_newcastle/2014/02/daily-pureland-practice.html accessed 3/11/15

Where do you begin?

1. Get in touch with the Amida Order and ask for a mentor from within the Order who will link you into the broader Sangha and who can support you in your efforts. You could also ask if there are any other known practitioners nearby.

2. See if you can find a friend (or two) who'll help you to set up your meetings. It is much easier to set up a group with two people – even if your friend just agrees to support you for the first few months. Your friend would need to be sympathetic to your intention but they don't have to be Buddhist – they could help by making tea when people arrive, or by joining in the chanting or reading out a passage from a Dharma book. A few of our Amida-shu groups started with the initiating person being supported by a non-Buddhist colleague or spouse, and some of them still operate very successfully in this way.

3. Have a think about what format you'd like your initial meeting to take. Will it be an informal get together to talk about what you might want to do in future meetings? Would you like to take the lead, or have a more flat structure with everyone taking equal responsibility for the group? Will you focus on practice, study or both? Here are a few ideas:

    •   Start the group with ten minutes of silent meditation and then read an extract from a book by Dharmavidya and discuss it.
    •   Listen to a Dharma talk (from online) followed by a bring and share meal.

- Follow the morning or evening service in the *Nien Fo Book* (or simplify it by choosing a few elements).
- Study the Introduction to Pureland Buddhism Course together.[40]

4. Think about where you'll find people who might want to join you. You might want to put up a poster in your local newsagent, create an event on Facebook, email all your friends (and encourage them to forward it to their friends), put an ad in the local newspaper (local papers often also have an online 'What's On' section which is often free to use), call a few people you think might be interested or send out a press release to local papers and radio.

5. Where will you hold your meetings? Many of us begin by holding groups in our own homes, but this isn't always appropriate. You might want to hire a room in a local church or complementary health centre, or meet in a coffee shop. Different venues will have pros and cons. Make sure there is a way of making people feel welcome wherever you hold your meeting – with tea and coffee available, a toilet people can use etc.

6. Decide how often you'd like to meet and set a few dates. In our experience these new groups take some time to settle down and grow and so it's helpful to begin with an attitude of patience. Here in Malvern we held six months of weekly meetings before our first few people 'stuck', and now four years on we have maybe thirty or forty

---

[40] http://courses.zentherapyinternational.com/ ?q=page/welcome-ITP

regular practitioners (and a temple!). It might help to view the prescribed time for practice and reflection as helpful for you, even if you're the only one who turns up. There are various reasons for slow growth – it's easier to join an established group than a small new one, the time needs to be right for people and so it can be six months between them first hearing about you and making it through the door, Pureland practice and theology can be more 'alien' to people than simple sitting meditation, etc. Use this time at the beginning to continue to deepen your own practice, and hand the rest over to Amida.

7. Enjoy your first meeting! You might be nervous or self-conscious – that's okay. Some people will like Pureland practice and some will find other groups or practices that are more suited to them – that's okay. You might make mistakes – that's okay. The most important bit is turning up and welcoming others – the rest will come with time.

8. Make a mailing list so you can keep in touch with people who express interest or who come along (always asking for permission before you add them). There are online packages like Mailchimp which allow you to write newsletters for free as long as you have less than a certain number of subscribers. Encourage your members to sign up for our main Amida-shu newsletter Whispers from the Bamboo Grove as a way of keeping in touch with the whole Sangha.

9. Allow the group to grow as it wants to grow. When people ask to meet more regularly, consider meeting more regularly. Try to give people responsibility and ownership as soon as you can (i.e. doing the washing up or helping with advertising the group) – people like to be helpful, and it also helps the group to feel more like a

community than a class. Keep in touch with your contact from Amida-shu and try to arrange visits to other Amida-shu groups whenever possible.

10. See everything that happens as an opportunity to learn about yourself and about the world. Make sure you get support if dilemmas arise, and make space for fun as well as for study and practice. Practise leaning on others as well as being there for others to lean on. Continue to be guided by Amida and remember that you're not in charge, the Buddhas are!

As they say in the twelve-step Traditions (which are designed to help keep groups healthy) 'Our common welfare should come first; personal recovery depends upon [group] unity'. Our personal spiritual well-being depends upon the health of the Sangha as a whole, and as our Sanghas grow and mature there are often inevitable difficulties between members or groups of members which can lead to friction or even schisms. This is how it has been throughout the history of Buddhism and of other religions and organisations of any kind. When this happens it is helpful to remember that we are bombu beings – we don't always act with wisdom, patience and compassion and so we can't expect others to do so either. Take refuge in the Sangha, and remember that the other two jewels are there when you need them!

I have received countless riches through taking refuge in the Sangha. We've spent countless hours listening to each other, working on joint projects and practising together in various shrine rooms, living rooms and gardens. We've also been through some pretty tough times together and this has deepened the sense of fellowship and the feelings of love and fondness I feel for my Sangha brothers and sisters. I hope that in time you might come to feel a little bit of this too.

Appendix B: How to connect with the Amida Sangha
Satyavani

At the time of writing there are Amida-shu Sanghas in Canada, Hawaii, Belgium, Scotland, and in England in Birmingham, London and Malvern. There are also individuals practising in Holland, Israel, France, Australia, and in various parts of the UK.

You'll find the most up to date list of contact details (and some other useful links) on our webpage: www.amidamandala.com/connect.

You could also email kaspalita@amidatrust.com or satya@amidatrust.com if you have any questions about anything you've read in this book or if you'd like to make contact.

Appendix C: History and structure of the Amida Order

Dharmavidya

Amida-shu is a self-regulating community (Sangha) of persons whose primary religious practice is nembutsu. It is culturally and socially engaged. It has formal provisions for structure, continuity and governance, and in different countries it operates through different locally constituted organisations. Membership is by invitation. At its core is the Amida Order.

Origin

The Amida Order came into being in the summer of 1998 when three people took bodhisattva vows with Dharmavidya. Initially the intention was not so much to create a new Sangha as to allow those who wished to do so to affirm their commitment to full time Buddhist training in a socially engaged context. Over the intervening years the Sangha has developed and the Order has clarified its orientation and structure and given birth to Amida-shu.

Features

The position now, therefore, is that a religious order exists at the core of Amida-shu and this order has a number of distinctive features:

- The order embodies complete equality between men and women.
- There are alternative ordination tracks as well as lay membership permitting different lifestyles.
- Options exist for celibate, married, and non-celibate persons.
- The Order is politically aware and socially engaged.
- It develops individuals and teams.
- It is deeply respectful of its Asian origins, yet as a new foundation has organisational flexibility.
- It has its own code of precepts for ordained members.

The Order consists of members of Amida-shu who have (a) become ordained, or (b) perform important functions, roles, or responsibilities for or within Amida-shu, or have done so in the past. Entry is by invitation. New members are people who are aligned to the Amida-shu vision and whose life accords with basic Buddhist ethics, though it is not a requirement that lay members formally take particular precepts.

Orientation

The Order affirms the three fundamentals of Amida-shu: the trikaya nature of Buddha, the bombu nature of the adherent and the primacy of nembutsu amongst its religious practices. These points place it within the Pureland tradition of Mahayana Buddhism. From this position of clarity, the Order reaches out in friendship to all branches of Buddhism and beyond to other faith communities in the cause of inter-religious harmony. The religious vision of the head of the Order is in accord with the spiritual instinct of people of many faiths – that there are absolute, spiritual and practical levels to the religious vision that work in harmony together (trikaya); that ordinary people are acceptable as they are (bombu); and that the core religious activity is the heart calling out to the beyond and receiving a response (nembutsu).

Structure

The Order is structured in terms of 'tracks' and 'stages'.

Tracks: There are lay and ordained members. The ordained members live according to a religious rule. Lay members have broad ethical guidelines. Among the ordained there are two ordination tracks. Those following the *ministry track* tend to live settled lives developing Dharma activities in their area, performing religious services, and getting socially engaged amidst their local population. Those following the *amitarya track* live mobile lives in mutually supportive community more like the traditional Buddhist friar (*bhikshu*). Ministers can be married or single and there is no restriction on them entering into relationships, so long as they do so in an ethical way. Married persons can only follow the amitarya track, however, if both members of the couple do so together, or the partner is wholly supportive. Single persons committing to the amitarya life are committing to a celibate lifestyle throughout their initial training of approximately three to four years. These arrangements, which are a distinctive feature of this order, mean that there are ordination routes for all three categories – celibates, married people practising together, and persons married to non-participants.

Offices: The Order has a number of functional offices, currently: Head of the Order, Deputy, Secretary, Archivist, Registrar, and Peacemaker. These may be held by lay or ordained members.

Stages: Persons who become lay order members or ministers generally begin by becoming members of Amidashu and engaging fully in its activities over a period of years. If they in due course assume a position of responsibility they may be invited to become a lay order member (*mitra*) or to ordain as a gankonin. Somebody who has worked as a gankonin for a number of years and for whom this work has become their full time occupation may be subsequently ordained as a minister. Those who aspire to become amitaryas begin by becoming residents at an Amida community and living the life of a trainee. When their intention to ordain has become clear, the trainee will be called a postulant. Postulancy generally lasts about one year. After first ordination this person becomes a novice. Novitiate usually lasts three years before full ordination.

At the time of writing there are, in the Amida Order, four acharyas. Acharya means teacher. Teaching responsibilities may be assumed by any member of the Order according to circumstance, but special recognition may also be given to persons who have been Order members for an extended period (at least ten years), who function as leading teachers and have disciples within the Order. Three of the acharyas are amitaryas and the other is a minister.

Training

Ordained members of the Order engage in on-going religious formation. This is a training that equips them to carry out the work of the Order, and which, more generally, brings out the best in people, equips them with enhanced life-skills, promotes social sensitivity, brings out leadership potential, deepens fellow feeling and compassion, and enables the members of the Order to work together in creative teams on a great diversity of activities.

Lifestyle

Being a member of the Order means devoting one's life to Dharma work within the frame of Buddhist ethics. It is a life of deep fellowship and mutual support with other Order members that reaches a particular intensity and intimacy. Although the internal structures of the Order may change over time and individuals may change their status within the Order after careful consideration, the commitment to Order membership itself, past initial probationary stages, is intended to be permanent.

Appendix D: Summary of Faith and Practice

by Dharmavidya, inspired by Honen's Ichimai Kishomon

For those having a karmic affinity with Amitabha Buddha wishing to practise a religious life in truly simple faith, freeing themselves of sophistication and attachment to all forms of cleverness, the method of opening oneself to Amitabha's grace is the practice of Nien Fo with body, speech and mind, particularly verbal recitation of 'Namo Amida Bu'. This is not something done as a form of meditation, nor is it based on study, understanding and wisdom, or the revelation of deep meaning. Deep meaning is indeed there for the nembutsu is a window through which the whole universe of Buddha's teaching can be perceived in all its depth, but none of this is either necessary or even helpful to success in the practice. Rather such study cultivates secondary faculties to be held separate from the mind of practice itself.

The primary practice requires only one essential: realise that you are a totally foolish being who understands nothing, but who can with complete trust recite 'Namo Amida Bu'; know that this will generate rebirth in the Pure Land, without even knowing what rebirth in the Pure Land truly is. This is the practice for ignorant beings and ignorance is essential for its accomplishment. This practice automatically encompasses the three minds and the mind of contrition as a fourth. To pursue something more profound or more sophisticated, or to have a theory, or to think that understanding will yield greater enlightenment than this is to be mislead and to fall back into self-power whereby the whole practice is spoilt. However wise, learned or skilled you may be, set it aside and be the foolish being completely in the performance of the practice. Nothing else is required and anything else is too much. Faith and practice cannot be differentiated.

The Buddha-body is delineated by the precepts. How deficient we are by comparison! By our daily difficulty in the preceptual life, we awaken to the presence of the myriad karmic obstacles without which we would already perceive the land of love and bliss, we would be as the vow-body of Buddha. Thus we know in experience that we are foolish beings of wayward passion. This knowledge of our condition is part of the essential basis when it gives rise to contrition. Thus all obstacles become impediments to faith unless we experience contrition and letting go. Saving grace, as was made clear by Shan Tao's dream and advice to Tao Cho, only comes through the sange-mon.

If you can perform the practice in this simple minded way, Amida will receive you and you may fear for nothing since all is completely assured. Dwelling in this settled faith you may then use your secondary faculties, your knowledge and skills and accumulated experience, as tools for helping all sentient beings. But do not then think that anything of relevance to your own salvation is thereby accomplished, nor that you are making something of yourself. Whatever merit there may be in your actions of this kind, immediately and

286

totally dedicate it to the benefit of others, that they may enter the Pure Land and that you yourself may not be encumbered by consciousness of virtue which will only contaminate the practice. As Honen says, 'without pedantic airs, fervently recite the Name.'

Appendix E: Meal time and incense offering verses

Meal time verses

Infinite benefits bless the breakfast food,
all beings profit greatly therefrom
Since the results are limitless and wonderful,
the pleasure is ours for eternity.

This food is the gift of the whole universe:
the earth, the sky, all sentient beings.
In this food is much joy, much suffering, much hard work.
We accept this food so that we may follow the path of
    practice,
and help all beings everywhere.

The first bite is to cut off delusion,
the second bite is to grow in faith,
the third bite is to help all beings.
We pray that all may be enlightened.
We pray for peace in this world,
and the cessation of all misfortune.

The Buddha invites us to eat in mindfulness,
of the food, the earth, the world around us.
We pray that our minds may not become dull,
nor our attention scattered,
and that we may realize the deep significance of life.

Incense offerings

(The first verse may be used for tea or flower offerings,
with appropriate words inserted.)

In gratitude we offer this incense
to all Buddhas and Bodhisattvas
throughout space and time.
May it be as fragrant as earth herself
reflecting our careful efforts,
our whole-hearted awareness,
and the fruit of understanding
slowly ripening.
May we and all beings be
companions of Buddhas and Bodhisattvas,
May we awaken from forgetfulness,
and realise the Pure Land.

The fragrance of this incense
permeates our practice centre,
and goes forth to worlds beyond.
In the sincerity of our training
the Sanghakaya is revealed.
Hearts and minds bow in gratitude.
Offerings multiply like the action,
of the all good one,
and the light that knows no obstacle
fills the Dharma realm.

Glossary of terms

Acharya (Sanskrit) – a Buddhist teacher. In Amida-shu, an ordained minister or amitarya who is recognised by the Head of the Order as a senior teacher.

Amida Buddha – the Buddha of unlimited light and unlimited life. Shakyamuni Buddha told the story of Amida Buddha who existed many kalpas before him.

Amida-shu – the name we give our school of Pureland Buddhism, inspired by many of the great Pureland ancestors and founded by Dharmavidya David Brazier.

Amitarya (Sanskrit) – literally 'Amida's noble person'. A word used in our tradition to describe people who have committed fully to the amitarya vows, including vows on living in community, being free to travel wherever you are needed, and celibacy vows during the training period. If you feel called to become an amitarya you first become a postulant (an amitarya in training) and undergo a period of spiritual training before being ordained.

Aspirant – a person recognised as aspiring to become a gankonin (Buddhist priest).

Avalokiteshvara (Sanskrit) – the Sanskrit word for Quan Shi Yin, the Bodhisattva of Compassion.

Bodhisattva (Sanskrit) – Bodhisattvas are inspired by the Buddhas and, although not yet Buddhas themselves, have great compassion and dedicate themselves to helping all sentient beings.

Bombu (Japanese) – a foolish being of wayward passion (i.e. all of us). As bombu beings we put ourselves in relationship with Amida Buddha and trust that if we say the nembutsu our rebirth in the Pureland is guaranteed.

Buddha (Sanskrit) – an enlightened being. Often used to mean Shakyamuni Buddha, the historical Buddha, who lived in India 2500 years ago.

Buddhakshetra (Sanskrit) – literally 'Buddha field', also known as a Pure Land. This is the field of influence of a Buddha. Around each Buddha there develops a Buddhakshetra. Devout Buddhists pray to be reborn in one so as to have the optimum opportunity to learn and practice the Dharma. See also: Pure Land and Sukhavati.

Chih quan (Chinese) – means 'peaceful seeing'. We sit quietly and whatever comes up, whether thoughts, feelings or physical sensations, we make an offering of it to the Buddha who gladly accepts whatever we offer. We are left with a sense of deepening peace. This meditation is usually used after nei quan.

Contrition – a deep feeling of regret and sadness when we fully realise the harmful consequence of our actions, whether intended or otherwise. Not to be confused with 'beating ourselves up' which is when we start to use our feelings of shame as a prop to our identity and start clinging to them or putting energy into them to keep them alive.

Dharma (Sanskrit) – The teachings of the Buddha. Also sometimes used to mean 'things as they are' or 'what is true'. One of the three jewels.

Dharmakara (Sanskrit) – the king in the Larger Pureland Sutra – the story Shakyamuni Buddha told to Ananda when Ananda noticed he was glowing. Dharmakara was inspired by the Buddha Lokeshvararaja and went on to eventually become Amida Buddha.

Dharmakaya (Sanskrit) – one of the three bodies of the Buddha (trikaya). Dharmakaya is the infinite unknowable quality of the Buddha – something we can't have a direct experience of with our finite bodies and minds.

Dukkha (Sanskrit) – the Sanskrit word used to mean affliction or suffering. The first of the Four Noble Truths.

The Four Noble Truths – the first teaching the Buddha gave and one that he repeated through the decades of his Dharma. For Dharmavidya's interpretation of the Four Noble Truths see his book, *The Feeling Buddha*, and subsequent writings.

Gankonin (Japanese neologism) – the word used in our tradition to describe a person who has been ordained and taken vows (also known as a Buddhist priest). Sangha members interested in this path first become an aspirant and after a period of training may be ordained as a gankonin. It can be a stage on the way to becoming a minister.

Honen Shonin – (1133–1212) Japanese Buddhist sage, and founder of Jodo Shu, the first Independent Pureland school in Japan.

Jodo-Shu (Japanense) – the school of Buddhism founded by Honen Shonin.

Jodo-Shinshu (Japanese) – the school of Buddhism founded by Shinran Shonin, one of Honen's disciples. Currently the largest Pureland school in Japan.

Karma (Sanskrit) – the Buddhist idea that intentional action sows seeds that ripen in the future, either as internal mental states or worldly circumstance.

Lokeshvararaja (Sanskrit) – the Buddha encountered by Dharmakara and who inspired him to take his vows and become Amida Buddha.

Mahayana Buddhism – one of the main two branches of Buddhism (the other is Theravada) practised widely in China, Japan, Korea, Tibet and Taiwan. Made up of a collection of Buddhist schools including Zen, Tibetan and Pureland Buddhism.

Minister – a fully ordained priest in Amida-shu (see also, Gankonin).

Naikan (Japanese) – see nei quan.

Namo Amida Bu – the nembutsu – saying the name of Amida Buddha. In Japan they say Namu Amida Butsu, and in China Namo Omito Fo.

Nei quan (Chinese) – insight meditation, especially a spiritual exercise where we focus on three questions: 'Whave I received, what have I offered in return and what trouble has my existence caused?'

Nembutsu (Japanese) – the practice of saying 'Namo Amida Bu'. In the Larger Pureland Sutra it says that anyone who hears the name of Amida Buddha will be reborn in his Pureland. Honen asks us to recite the nembutsu so it is audible to our own ears.

Nirmanakaya (Sanskrit) – one of the three bodies of the Buddha (trikaya). This is when the Buddha appears to us in physical form – for example, Shakyamuni Buddha who lived on this earth 2500 years ago. Also known as the transformation body.

Pali – the language in which the scriptures of the Theravada School of Buddhism are recorded.

Postulant – the word which designates someone who aspires to become an amitarya within the Amida-shu and who is in training.

Precepts – ethical ideals such as 'do not kill' which we aspire to as Buddhists. Ordained people in our Order 'take precepts' in their Ordination ceremony and make a formal vow to keep them as best they can.

The Pure Land – see Buddakshetra. Generally, in Pureland Buddhism, this refers to the realm of bliss that surrounds Amida Buddha. This is described in great detail in the Larger Pure Land Sutra as a place where there are cool pools of bathing water, jewelled trees, a beautiful melodious music etc. Some Amida-shu Buddhists see the Pure Land as a real place where they will be reborn after death. Others see it as a vision of an ideal society where we care for each other and the environment, and which we can start working towards right now in this life.

Pureland Buddhism or just **Pureland** – the form of Buddhism popularised by Honen in the 12th century in Japan, based on the vows made by Amida Buddha.

Quan Shi Yin (Chinese)- the Bodhisattva of Compassion, also known as Avalokiteshvara.

Refuge – taking refuge is a central practice for all Buddhists and gives us a sense of security and faith. Most Buddhists take refuge in the three jewels – Shakyamuni Buddha, the Dharma and the Sangha. Amida-shu Buddhists also take refuge in Amida Buddha and the Pure Land.

Rupa (Sanskrit) – the power that an object has to draw our attention, or an object that is highly charged with personal meaning. We also speak of Buddha statues being 'Buddha rupas' as they represent the Buddha.

Samadhi (Sanskrit) – a state of peaceful concentration, or consummate vision.

Sambhogakaya (Sanskrit) – one of the three bodies of the Buddha (trikaya). This quality comes to us through dreams or visions, and is the body of the Buddha that we can connect to through spiritual experiences. Also known as the bliss body.

Samsara (Sanskrit) – the continuing cycle of birth and death, the world of karma, and the worldly world.

Sange-mon (Japanese) – can be translated as the 'gate of contrition', which we all need to walk through in order to find grace. A genuine experience of our limitations and failings points us towards Amida Buddha, who accepts us just as we are.

Sangha (Sanskrit) – the community of people who follow the Buddha's teachings. One of the three jewels.

Sanskrit – the primary language used by Indian Mahayana Buddhists.

Shakyamuni Buddha (Sanskrit) – literally 'sage of the Shakyas'. The Buddha (born as a prince, Siddhartha Gautama) who lived 2500 years ago in India and who founded Buddhism as a religion.

Sukhavati (Sanskrit) – literally 'sweet or blissful land'. The Pure Land of Amida Buddha. See also: Buddhakshetra.

Sutra (Sanskrit) – the sacred scriptures that contain the discourses of the Buddha (Sutta in Pali).

Theravada Buddhism – literally 'path of the elders'. The branch of Buddhism which uses the teachings of the Pali Canon. The dominant religion in Sri Lanka, Thailand, Cambodia and Laos and with practitioners across the world.

The Three Jewels – the Buddha, the Dharma and the Sangha.

The Three Minds – a teaching in Pureland Buddhist texts important in the writings of the 7th Century Master Shan Tao. These are sincere mind (being honest and free of hypocrisy), deep mind (a willingness to trust that we are supported) and a mind that offers merit (also known as a longing mind or a mind that reaches out towards Amida Buddha).

Trikaya (Sanskrit) – a way of describing the different forms that the Buddha takes (or the different 'bodies' of the Buddha). These are: dharmakaya, manifestation of ultimate truth; sambhogakaya, manifestation as spiritual presence and nirmanakaya, manifestation as physical appearance.

Zazen (Japanese) – Zen meditation practice. Often 'just sitting' where you sit upright and quietly on a zafu (a meditation cushion) without putting energy into anything else (thinking, for example).

Further reading

What follows is a mix of recommended Pureland and other Buddhist texts and our personal favourite books. We've put an asterix by the few we'd suggest you start with. Enjoy.

Atone, Joji *The Promise of Amida's Buddha: Honen's Path to Bliss* (2011) Wisdom Publications

Bloom, Alfred *Essential Shinran: The Path of True Entrusting* (2006) World Wisdom Books

Bikkhu Bodhi (Translator) *The Connected Discourses of the Buddha: A Translation of the Samyutta Nikaya* (2003) Wisdom Publications

Bikkhu Bodhi (Translator) *The Numerical Discourses of the Buddha: A Complete Translation of the Anguttara Nikaya (Teachings of the Buddha)* (2012) Wisdom Publications

Brazier, Caroline *The Other Buddhism: Amida Comes West* (2007) O Books

Brazier, David *Buddhism Is A Religion* (2014) Woodsmoke Press

Brazier, David *Not Everything Is Impermanent* (2013) Woodsmoke Press

Brazier, David *Zen Therapy: Transcending the Sorrows of the Human Mind* New York : John Wiley & Sons (1995)

*Brazier, David *The Feeling Buddha: A Buddhist Psychology of Character, Adversity and Passion* (2002) Robinson

*Brazier, David *Who Loves Dies Well* (2007) O Books

Brazier, David *Love and its Disappointment* (2009) O Books

Chadwick, David *Crooked Cucumber: The Life and Teachings of Suzuki Shunryu* (2000) Broadway Books

Fitzgerald, Joseph A. *Honen the Buddhist Saint: Essential Writings and Official Biography* (2006) World Wisdom Books

Keenan, Terrance *Zen Encounters With Loneliness* (2014) Wisdom Publications

Kornfield, Jack *After the Ecstasy, the Laundry* (2000) Rider

Bikkhu Nanamoli (Translator) Bikkhu Bodhi (Translator) *The Middle Length Discourses of the Buddha: A Translation of the Majjhima Nikaya (Teachings of the Buddha)* (1995) Wisdom Publications

Paraskevopoulos, John *Call of the Infinite: The Way of Shin Buddhism* (2009) Sophia Perennis et Universalis

Shapiro, Rami *Recovery – The Sacred Art: The Twelve Steps as Spiritual Practice* (2009) Skylight Paths Publishing

Suzuki, Shunryu *Zen Mind, Beginner's Mind* (2005) Weatherhill

Welwood, John *Toward a Psychology of Awakening: Buddhism, Psychotherapy, and the Path of Personal and Spiritual Transformation* (2002) Shambhala

Unno, Taitetsu *Shin Buddhism: Bits of Rubble Turn into Gold* (2002) Harmony

Unno, Taitetsu *River of Fire, River of Water* (1998) Image

Walshe, Maurice (Translator), Sumedho, Ajahn (Foreword) *The Long Discourses of the Buddha: A Translation of the Digha Nikaya* (1995) Wisdom Publications

Namo Amida Bu

Lightning Source UK Ltd.
Milton Keynes UK
UKOW06f0920041215

264064UK00003B/11/P